Writing about Literature
A Guide for the Student Critic

second edition

W.F. Garrett-Petts

Writing
about
Literature

A Guide for the Student Critic

second edition

W.F. Garrett-Petts

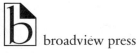 broadview press

Library and Archives Canada Cataloguing in Publication

Garrett-Petts, W. F. (William Francis), 1954–
    Writing about literature : a guide for the student critic / W.F. Garrett-Petts. —2nd ed.

Includes bibliographical references and index.
ISBN 978-1-55111-743-0

    1. Criticism—Authorship.   2. Literature—History and criticism—Theory, etc.
3. Academic writing.   I. Title.

PE1479.C7G377 2013   808.06'68   C2013–901049–1

Broadview Press is an independent, international publishing house, incorporated in 1985.

We welcome comments and suggestions regarding any aspect of our publications—please feel free to contact us at the addresses below or at broadview@broadviewpress.com.

North America
PO Box 1243, Peterborough, Ontario, Canada K9J 7H5
2215 Kenmore Ave., Buffalo, New York, USA 14207
Tel: (705) 743-8990; Fax: (705) 743-8353
email: customerservice@broadviewpress.com

UK, Europe, Central Asia, Middle East, Africa, India, and Southeast Asia
Eurospan Group, 3 Henrietta St., London WC2E 8LU, United Kingdom
Tel: 44 (0) 1767 604972; Fax: 44 (0) 1767 601640
email: eurospan@turpin-distribution.com

Australia and New Zealand
NewSouth Books
c/o TL Distribution, 15-23 Helles Ave., Moorebank, NSW, Australia 2170
Tel: (02) 8778 9999; Fax: (02) 8778 9944
email: orders@tldistribution.com.au

www.broadviewpress.com

Copy-edited by Martin Boyne. Designed by Zack Taylor, Metapolis.

Broadview press acknowledges the financial support of the Government of Canada through the Canada Book Fund for our publishing activities.

This book is printed on paper containing 100% post-consumer fibre.

PRINTED IN CANADA

Contents

CHAPTER 6
Some Final Words on Writing about Literature   149

Acknowledgements

It is impossible to acknowledge by name all the teachers and scholars whose example has helped shape my sense of what it takes to become a successful literary critic. No doubt I've echoed here advice first heard from such exemplary teachers as E.D. Blodgett, Chris Bullock, Frank Davey, Sherrill Grace, Paul Hjartarson, Anthony Jenkins, Andrea Lunsford, James Marino, Shirley Neuman, Colin Partridge, and Laurie Ricou—all of whom have had profound influence upon the way I read and write about and teach literature (though, as it is commonly said, none should be held responsible for any mistakes or misrepresentations made here). Most of what follows, however, has been worked out over twenty-five years of trial and error with my own students, whose generous participation and feedback have contributed immeasurably to this book.

Five of those students have contributed directly, adding their voices to the text: Michelle Demers, Debbie Endean, Lydia Marston, Ryan Miller, and Charlotte Tetreau. It gives me great personal pleasure to showcase their work.

I am also grateful to those fellow teachers and literary critics whose work is reproduced here—and who believed in this project enough to share new essays written or revised expressly for *Writing about Literature*: Tina Blue, Alice Farley, Helen Gilbert, Eric Gislason, Michael Jarrett, Katherine Sutherland, and David Wilson-Okamura. My special thanks go to Harold Kolb, Jr.; his personal encouragement, scrupulous scholarship, and superb knowledge of the field (as evidenced by his interview and essay contributions) helped me refine my intuitions and convictions regarding how we might rethink the literature class as a place to teach writing. New to the second edition is a chapter of reading and writing about poetry—and here I want to thank Robert Kroetsch for sharing not only a poem to study but also a remarkable interview on the writing of that poem.

Many other friends and colleagues have contributed suggestions, comments, criticism, and encouragement. I thank in particular Katherine Alexander, Neil Besner, Rick Coe, Sandra Dueck, Brenton Faber, Henry Hubert, Russ Hunt, Bernard Igwe, Anthony Paré, Cathy Schryer, Christine Skolnick, Philippa Spoel, and the discussion group members of the Canadian Association for the Study of Language and Learning.

I would be remiss in not thanking Don LePan, President of Broadview Press, for first suggesting and then fostering this book;

Writing about Literature: A Guide for the Student Critic

Dennis Keusch, for his wonderfully ironic illustrations rendered in the style of Blumenschein; Martin Boyne, Laurna and Richard Tallman, Emily Hope, and Bronwen Scott for their keen-eyed copy-editing; production editors Barbara Conolly and Allison LaSorda, for accommodating my sometimes overly fastidious layout requests; Zack Taylor for his design work on the second edition, and Bonnie Farris of ergo² for her initial design and typesetting; Joan Eadie for the expert indexing; Heidi Standell, of Broadview's Calgary office, for answering all my e-mail inquiries and facilitating long-distance lines of communication; and Marjorie Mather for encouraging the second edition of this book. My thanks also to Robert Panzer, Executive Director of VAGA, New York; the staff at the University of Virginia Library; and Iris Snyder, Special Collections, University of Delaware Library, all of whom were helpful in tracking down copyright information regarding permission to reproduce E.L. Blumenschein's 1898 illustrations. The copies were taken with permission from the collection at the University of British Columbia Library, and digital image processing was provided by Alan Fedorak of Fedorak Photography.

Specific copyright acknowledgements for the print quotations are listed as follows:

Alice Hall Farley (a.k.a. Alice Hall Petry). "Crane's Bride Comes to Yellow Sky." Originally published in *The Explicator* 42 (Fall 1983): 45-47. Reprinted with permission of the Helen Dwight Reid Educational Foundation. Published by Heldref Publications, 1319 Eighteenth St. N.W., Washington, D.C. 20036-1802. Copyright ©1983.

Thomas A. Fink's table is from "Reading Deconstructively in the Two-Year College Literature Class," originally published in *Teaching English in the Two Year College* 12 (February 1985): 64-71. Copyright ©1985 by the National Council of Teachers of English. Reprinted with permission.

Clifford Geertz's extract is taken from *The Interpretation of Cultures* by Clifford Geertz. Copyright ©1973 by Basic Books, Inc. Reprinted by permission of Basic Books, a member of Perseus Books, L.L.C.

I am grateful to the Social Sciences and Humanities Research Council of Canada and to Thompson Rivers University for research grants that, though originally earmarked for other research projects, provided important background material incorporated into the present book.

Finally, this book is dedicated to the three women in my life— to my daughters, Kate and Samantha, whose love of reading and writing gives me joy; and to my wife, Nancy, whose presence steadfastly maintains, *contra* Derrida, that there *is* something outside the text.

Preface to the Second Edition— to the Instructor

In an article entitled "One, Two, Three," rhetorician and social critic Richard Lanham poses three important questions:

> One: *What is the relationship between teaching literature and teaching composition?*
>
> Two: *Should English departments take an interest in teaching composition?*
>
> Three: *How does question one relate to question two?* (14)

I take it for granted that few of us working in departments of English are unaware of the rivalries and inequities that obtain between those teaching in these ostensibly allied fields. While this is not the place to rehearse a full historical analysis of the gap between literature and composition instruction, I think it important to acknowledge that an awareness of this gap has motivated the approach taken here: *Writing about Literature: A Guide for the Student Critic* is based on the premise that, in teaching students to write literary criticism, we must find creative, pedagogically sound ways of relating question one to question two. My working assumption is that composition instruction does have a place in the traditional literature course; indeed, in light of recent scholarship in genre theory, workplace writing, and writing in the disciplines, I would argue that the literature course provides an ideal pedagogical space in which to teach students the conventions of what is commonly being called "discipline-specific" writing.

By way of explaining what I mean by discipline-specific writing, let me begin with a brief background note. Every book has its own story, and this one began over 20 years ago, shortly before I accepted my first full-time teaching appointment. One of my former teachers, Colin Partridge, advised me that the nature of writing had changed considerably in his lifetime. "Once," he noted, "we could speak confidently of 'Standard English,' that shared reservoir of vocabulary and linguistic structures." Today, with competition from electronic media, and added competition from highly specialized academic and business discourses, students generally enter and leave the universities with no overflowing reservoir of language resources. "In the twentieth century," he told me, "people learn their literacy skills on the job. In effect, before learning to write, our students must first choose a profession." He had just designed a new Business Communications course for cooperative education students, and he was busy working out the implications of what today is called workplace writing.

His advice hit home when, several months later, I was asked to teach a section of business writing in a Social Service Worker program. At the time I had an MA in English (with a concentration in literary studies and composition), but my academic training had not prepared me for the kind of writing my students needed to learn. Their workplace writing required detailed analysis of social conventions and formats. We spent a good deal of the time quizzing guest speakers on the kind of writing they did. About how to write a good report. About what constituted a good letter, and what to do when faced with the task of communicating bad or unwelcome news. We came to regard workplace writing as a tool to solve a definable set of problems.

At the same time I was teaching two sections of college-transfer English (a standard freshman English course). I was struck by the differences. For one thing, any instruction I offered regarding critical writing required much less "field work." After all, I was a trained (and published) critic, and thus I could speak to my students with some authority. I spoke for the profession. We never invited other critics in for class interviews; I provided little historical, institutional, or social context for the study of literature. Our focus was on the texts, not the contexts.

Looking back on the two sets of students, I suspect the results were, even then, predictable: my Social Service Worker students learned the conventions of writing more quickly (and with more enthusiasm) than the college-transfer students in my first-year English course. Unlike the Social Service Worker students, my freshman English students had not chosen literary criticism as either a profession or an avocation. I'm sure that I must have made a case for literary study—and I know we said a great deal about the short stories, novels, and poetry—but I probably did little to bring *the field* of literary criticism alive. For my students, reading and writing about literature was a ritual of the classroom, something far removed from the work of actual critics. Our discussions may have emulated those of practised critics, that is, we explored issues of authorial intent, historical context, genre, style, and interpretation; but something was lost in the translation from classroom talk to essay writing.

Classroom discussion creates its own context, where one interpretation variously collides, colludes, or converses with others. The dynamic of such critical exchange can entertain and seduce even the initially uninterested student. Writing the critical essay, though, presents a different set of challenges. Writing can seem a lonely, isolated, and even isolating experience. Too often the written essay lacks life, energy, and purpose. It pales in comparison with the lively classroom discussion that may have preceded it. Here, then, is the great irony of our field: while most traditional English classes spend a great deal of time discussing literature, relatively little direct instruction is offered in how to write about literature. Yet the ability to write critical essays remains our principal criterion for judging success. The student who cannot write a conventionally well-crafted and critically informed essay is, quite simply, not speaking the language of literary critics, or of the teacher.

What I've learned as a teacher, and what this book offers, is some proven strategies for making the critical context both visible and relevant. Literature students may not need to choose literary criticism as a profession, but they do have a need (and a right) to understand why we in English studies do what we do—and what can be gained from practising the arts of critical reading and writing.

Initiating Students into Literary Study

It is generally recognized that literary texts are best read in their social, historical, and critical contexts. Yet, ironically, writing about literature is often learned in something of a social, historical, and critical vacuum. If your students feel at all confused or frustrated by the way academics talk and write, they are not alone. Most undergraduate students tend to approach the writing of critical essays as outsiders uninitiated in the disciplinary assumptions, approaches, and models that shape successful writing in the field. In fact, literature is often taught with only passing reference to the history, organization, and assumptions informing the critical essay. Students are taught how to *read* about literature, but the secrets of how to *write* about literature are often imparted indirectly, or are left to be picked up in their senior years (when, if they decide to take further English courses, they begin to study the body of critical literature surrounding the primary texts). Unlike creative writing courses, where students read examples of fine poetry or prose fiction as models to be emulated, literature courses ask students to spend most of their time studying forms they will never be asked to write.

But why wouldn't literary studies offer explicit instruction in essay writing?

There are numerous reasons for this apparent lack of attention to writing about literature. Most literature instructors do not see themselves as composition specialists, and therefore they spend relatively little instructional time on the form of the critical essay. Instructors often begrudge taking classroom time "away" from discussion of the literary texts. And some instructors fear that their students, at least at the first- and second-year levels, will be either unduly influenced or intimidated by professional critical interpretations.

In addition, and perhaps more troubling for those of us wishing to make students feel at home in the discipline, much of what we do as practising critics remains unexamined, even unconscious. We tend to take the general form of the critical essay for granted. As Richard Coe points out, "writers expert in particular genres are often incapable of describing the crucial features of the genre (and often give terribly incomplete and misleading advice to students or apprentices if asked to do so)" (158). Knowing "how" does not always mean one is able to explain "about"—though ideally the two are linked.

Those who take the field for granted tend to take the "sink or swim" attitude toward explicit writing instruction. Their students learn by doing, by adapting to the implied social, institutional, and disciplinary cues inculcated through classroom discussion and feedback on essays and exams. These students also learn, or fail to learn, by comparing notes with other students—and, if they are confident enough, by asking the right questions. Above all, students learn that reading, not writing, remains the primary focus of literary study.

A Brief History of English Studies

Reading and writing have necessarily existed together, but a review of twentieth-century English studies reveals an agonizingly extended effort to teach reading without writing. For at least the first half of the twentieth century, English studies fashioned itself as an anti-utilitarian field of study, one more concerned with introducing students to high art culture and the life of the imagination than with training students to develop technical writing skills. A relative newcomer to the college curriculum, "English" was first introduced in the nineteenth century as both an alternative to scientific rationalism and as a supplement to organized religion (in failing health by the late Victorian period, as Terry Eagleton explains). Like religion, the study of literature was (and to a lesser extent, still is) more about ritual, self-discovery, aesthetic involvement, and textual interpretation than about the generation of technically correct essays. From the nineteenth century on, the principal purpose of English has been to introduce students to the humanities: English "cultivate[s] a taste for reading as a form of intelligent recreation" (qtd. in Harris 126).

The last century has seen an increasing emphasis on disciplinary specialization. Although the "recreational" aspect of English studies lingers, for the most part it has given way to a professional or "disciplinary" focus. As Northrop Frye argued in a 1960 address,

| xv |

> In the university the relation of teacher and student is strictly subordinated to the authority of the subject being taught. In the university there is no longer any such thing as "education": there is only literature, chemistry, history, and similar subjects to be studied. (34)

Like those working in chemistry or history, we teachers of literature see ourselves as subject-area specialists. We are concerned that our students learn the subject matter, theories, and approaches of the discipline. Unlike other disciplines, however, English still carries its original "civilizing" mission of introducing students to the best that has been thought and known. The early idealism is still alive and well—but to some extent also in conflict with the pragmatic task of teaching essay-writing skills (see Hubert and Garrett-Petts).

For many English instructors, the whole idea of providing technical, "how-to" directions contradicts the implicit goal of helping students find their own way, of cultivating new levels of aesthetic response. As Jasper Neel notes (with his tongue lodged only slightly in his cheek), "Professors of literary interpretation will go to almost any length to avoid telling students what to do in their papers" (315). Although there are always exceptions, English instructors tend to bridle at the notion of providing too much technical advice. Students, instead, are referred to handbooks or to generic composition texts— or, as I noted above, are simply expected to "learn by doing."

I see elements of this same conflict in our discipline's love/hate relationship with "close reading." When we direct attention to "the words on the page," we are invoking the mantra of New Critical pedagogy. The ghosts of John Crowe Ransom, Cleanth Brooks, and Robert Penn Warren still haunt our discipline and, more importantly, they still guide contemporary critical practice. As Peter Rabinowitz notes, "Belief in close reading may be the nearest thing literary scholars have to a shared critical principle" (A40). While most of us are committed to the pedagogical goal of teaching students proven techniques for reading those words on the page, we remain wary of too much technique. Many of us share our students' suspicion that we can analyze a good story to death. English studies, it seems, is an academic discipline intent on preserving its "amateur" roots.

One reviewer of this book summarized the dilemma this way: "A large part of many students' struggle with the practice of critical analysis stems from their sense that analysing literature is alienating as well as difficult. Analysis appears to enforce detachment and work against the affective dimension of reading." The reviewer goes on to outline a familiar compromise, noting that the ideal English course not only teaches "students to write competent critical essays and familiarizes them with English studies as a discipline, but also introduces or reintroduces them to the notion of reading as a pleasure." I would add only that, if presented in a balanced and thoughtful manner, critical analysis and pleasurable reading need not be considered mutually exclusive activities. Ideally, one should enhance the other. Certainly it seems unfair to ask our students to write interpretative essays without first providing (1) an introduction to critical reading methods, (2) a clear sense of the critical context and audience, and (3) a range of exemplary models that they can follow.

Where does this leave our students? The good news is that things are changing. A new disciplinary self-consciousness about literary theory and a renewed emphasis on writing have combined to make us all more aware of how language-using communities work. As more has become known about the way "discourse communities" function, academics generally are becoming aware that we need to teach subjects *in context*. With some sense of urgency, English studies in particular has taken up the challenge of exploring how writing helps to constitute each discipline (or academic community).

If English studies began in the universities as a means of inculcating "educated" taste, judgement, and aesthetic norms, today it is arguably the most self-critical and pluralistic of the disciplines. It is also, in many ways, the most central of disciplines, taking as its subject not only the study of texts but also the study of interpretation itself. Understanding (1) the process of interpretation, (2) the critical, historical, and institutional contexts of interpretation, and (3) the forms through which we communicate our interpretations are today's crucial issues—ones that any serious student of literature must address.

This Book's Form and Philosophy

Writing about Literature is a hybrid text, part critical casebook and part rhetoric of criticism. The critical casebook (collections of critical essays on selected authors or works) is a familiar enough form—from Coles Notes to the Bedford Books series, Case Studies in Contemporary Criticism. Although undeniably useful, the critical collections and cribs tend to provide students with a hearsay version of literary criticism. The students hear about the importance of literary scholarship, and they read the results of such scholarship, but they are seldom invited to participate in hands-on research. For years I have heard students complain about the gap between published criticism and the critical writing they feel able to produce. The professional essays remain a kind of foreign language, something that others write, something that can be quoted but seldom emulated.

| xvii |

Casebooks traditionally offer little if any advice on how to think and write like a literary critic: on how you know a "good topic" from a mediocre one; on the values of the literary community; on what constitutes "evidence" in literary studies; on how to gather that evidence; on how to organize the essay; on questions of critical approach and methodology; on the kind of tone, voice, and specialized vocabulary peculiar to literary criticism; on how to quote and integrate those quotations—in short, on how to do "the work" of literary studies.

Rhetorics on "writing about literature," on the other hand, provide a detailed overview of the whole field, usually covering prose fiction, poetry, drama, and even film. Such texts fill a need, and I've often recommended them as resources to my own students. What I've found lacking, though, in these introductions to literature is some sense of the issues and excitement that first attracted me to English literature as a field of study. It seems in the nature of general introductions to smooth over the conflicts, the disagreements—in short, "the fun"—of literary debate and critical exchange.

Like casebooks, traditional rhetorics tend to offer little insight (or "insider knowledge") regarding the language, phrasing, and disciplinary attitudes of literary study. The student examples tend to be technically correct but not outstanding; the sections on how to construct a critical essay tend to rehearse the sort of generic advice one finds in most general composition texts—advice on "finding a topic," "writing a thesis statement," "documenting sources," etc. What gets left out of most texts is some indication of the underlying disciplinary values, history, traditions, and approaches that inform such choices. Students need to understand what makes some topics well suited to literary study and others better suited to, say, history or sociology. They also need to hear that contemporary literary studies is not all "sweetness and light," that English is an exciting, emotionally charged, and highly debated field of intellectual inquiry.

In *Writing about Literature*, I offer an alternative teaching and studying aid. A cross between a rhetoric and a casebook, this text provides clear, practical advice and accessible models for understanding and writing critical essays on literature—on prose fiction in particular. In Chapter 3, I lead students step-by-step through the process of writing a critical paper, transforming a sample failing effort into an example of first-class undergraduate work. While not exhaustive, the process demonstrates how a variety of critical approaches can enhance reading and generate new ways of thinking and writing about the text. Chapter 4 offers a collection of model essays, three by student writers and three by professional critics. Two of the professional essays are new, written especially for this book. In addition, the text features a selection of "field notes": professional and pedagogical statements designed to help students develop a sense of the kind of issues, attitudes, and practices that define English as a field of study.

To help focus the advice and give both a "casebook" feel and utility value to the text, Stephen Crane's classic short story "The Bride Comes to Yellow Sky" is included as first printed in 1898; in addition, most of the advice on composition and critical approaches refers to this story. The inclusion of Crane's story distinguishes *Writing about Literature* as more than a supplementary handbook separable from the other primary course materials. Instead, it is anticipated that instructors may want to use both the story and the accompanying models as vehicles for direct classroom instruction, perhaps early in the semester as an introduction to prose fiction analysis. Once they learn the principles of critical writing, students should be able to extend them, with guidance, to other literary forms and purposes.

New to the second edition is a chapter on reading and writing about poetry: this new chapter follows the casebook model, featuring a poem by Robert Kroetsch; a remarkable interview with the author, where he reflects on the composition of his poem and offers advice to students on reading poetry in general; a tool kit for student writers and field notes on prosody and poetic form; and model student responses echoing those provided in Chapter 3. In addition, all the model essays presented have been updated in the current MLA documentation style, and all Internet resources and recommended readings have been revised.

Taken as a whole, the text offers an implied alternative to the "coverage model" of literary instruction. Instead of moving from example to representative example, *Writing about Literature* provides enough resources for students to explore a single classic work and a contemporary poem in detail—and from multiple perspectives. The text takes seriously Douglas Lanier's advice that "the introductory literature class [should] introduce students to a range of critical strategies in an effort to demonstrate that a single text can be read differently by different interpretive communities" (202). Further, the compact length of the text should make it useful for students and attractive to instructors who want only a brief primer on the subject.

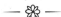

I'd like to end this preface with a word on what this book is *not*. It is neither an introduction to literary theory nor an exhaustive survey of critical approaches. Reference to reader-response criticism, feminist reading practices, close-reading strategies, New Historicism, myth criticism, Marxist criticism, postcolonial criticism, and deconstruction is tied to specific examples and demonstrations of critical practice. The emphasis is on practical application rather than on full theoretical explication. Those wishing their students to read more extensively in these areas can consult the list of excellent titles provided in the "Resources for Further Study" section that ends this book. What I *do* focus on here, especially in the first half of the book, is the rhetoric of writing undergraduate essays in literature. This is an insider's guide to the language, issues, approaches, styles, assumptions, and traditions that inform the writing of successful critical essays. That said, I make no pretence that I have covered *all* critical approaches or *all* possible issues. Such an ambition would exceed the scope of any primer—and probably test the patience of most readers. It is hoped instead that this book will raise important questions, offer useful answers and guidance, but still leave ample room for personal and classroom exploration. *Writing about Literature* lends an informed context to that exploration and seeks to ensure that your students' expression of critical response meets disciplinary conventions and expectations.

Preface to the Second Edition—
to the Student: An Introduction
to the Critical Conversation

What Is Academic Discourse?

Have you ever noticed how people in colleges and universities tend to "speak like books"? As members of an intellectual community, they have adopted a more formal way of talking (and thinking and writing) than you might expect to find elsewhere. Becoming an active and successful participant within a college or university means learning the *academic discourse* or language of the community. At first, such discourse may sound strange, even pretentious. But failing to learn it can have serious consequences. The language of any academic discipline reflects established community attitudes and values. When you don't use the right words and approaches, miscommunication occurs. You mark yourself as someone unfamiliar with the way things are normally written, said, and done. Cathy Copley explains it this way:

> Imagine someone new to sports trying to start a conversation with long-time sports fans: "So what do you think the Raiders will wear in their next game?" or "Was Martina Navratilova's last match cost-effective?" or "Which Knick do you think is the best dad?" This person just isn't asking the "right" questions, hasn't got sports talk straight. It's not a matter of wardrobe or accounting or good parenting; it's plays, scores, contracts, winners. If you want to join the conversation, those are the terms. ("Academic Writing")

Copley's examples are, of course, exaggerations. Few of us would make the kinds of category mistakes she alludes to here. "Sports talk" crosses all kinds of social lines, and most of us are familiar with its rules. Yet those entering the college English class for the first time are quite likely to feel out of place—at least at first. Like sports, joining the literary conversation involves *knowing how to ask the right questions*. You have to talk the talk as you learn to walk the walk.

Learning how things are done in a literature class is as much a matter of learning about community assumptions, genres, modes of expression, metaphors, traditions, and attitudes as it is about spelling, punctuation, and paragraph development. This book is designed to help you "come to terms" with critical discourse.

...READER RESPONSE THEORY...

...THE TEXT AS EVIDENCE...

...POSTMODERN LITERATURE...

...BLOCK QUOTATIONS...

Joining the Critical Conversation

The American critic Kenneth Burke likens the learning of new disciplines to entering a room where others are busily engaged in heated discussion:

> Imagine that you enter a parlor. You come late. When you arrive, others have long preceded you, and they are engaged in a heated discussion, a discussion too heated for them to pause and tell you exactly what it is about. In fact the discussion had already begun long before any of them got there, so that no one present is qualified to retrace for you all the steps that had gone before. You listen for a while, until you decide that you have caught the tenor of the argument; then you put in your oar. Someone answers; you answer him; another comes to your defense; another aligns himself against you, to either the embarrassment or gratification of your opponent, depending upon the quality of your ally's assistance. However, the discussion is interminable. The hour grows late, you must depart. And you do depart, with the discussion still vigorously in progress. (*Philosophy* III)

Most of us have experienced the kind of dislocation, even momentary alienation, that Burke describes. Burke's parlour and the average class-room have a lot in common. Both seem preoccupied with matters that began long before most of the people arrived. Both require time for the "guests" to catch on to the give and take of the ongoing conversation. Similarly, learning the language of literary criticism requires a kind of apprenticeship, a period of close listening and practice.

Unlike Burke's parlour or Copley's football stadium, however, the classroom contains at least one person "qualified to retrace for you ... [most] of the steps that had gone before": the instructor. Like a good host, the instructor can outline some of the stances taken, introduce the guests to one another, and perhaps even summarize what has been said and what issues have been addressed. But providing such information does not ensure that the newly arrived will feel able to jump in and participate right away. Only the most precocious or foolhardy would want to venture opinions or analyses in a room full of strangers, no matter how welcoming or stimulating the discussion—at least not until catching the drift and tenor of the conversation.

What most of us need to feel comfortable in such circumstances is more than a good host or even a sympathetic audience; what we need is enough *background knowledge* to enter the conversation with confidence. We can linger (or languish) long enough to learn the drift. We can monopolize the host, peppering her with questions. We can corner someone who came earlier and quiz him or her about *who* said *what* and *why*. Or we can combine all these approaches by

- listening closely to what is said,
- engaging in conversation whenever possible, and
- remaining confident that *eventually* we will contribute with ease.

This combination method is the one advocated in this book.

A Method for Learning Academic Discourse

To learn anything new we first need to be shown how something is done: we need clear *demonstrations*, whether they are in the form of classroom lectures, discussions, or written examples. At the same time we need to feel *engaged* in the demonstration: only when we feel involved in the demonstration do we move from the role of spectator to that of participant (and thus from passive observer to active learner). Finally, to feel involved, we need to understand what's at stake, what's expected, and what can be gained. We need to understand the full *social context* of learning. There's more to writing about literature than recounting a good interpretation (although *interpretation* is central to your task). Your success depends on whether you know

- your purpose
- your audience
- what should and should not be said
- why certain topics and approaches are better received than others
- where to look for evidence and support
- how best to express and organize your ideas

When you've come to terms with these six areas, you will be in a strong position to practice writing like a literary critic.

Throughout *Writing about Literature*, you'll find detailed demonstrations in the form of examples and model essays. To ensure engagement, I have

- restricted most of those examples and models to one famous short story and one contemporary poem,
- included the text of the story and the poem as a shared point of reference, and
- added a number of exercises designed to help you think and write critically.

In other words, once you have read the story and the poem, you should be in an excellent position to *engage* (and thus learn from) the exercises and examples provided.

The third component of learning, social context, is more difficult to put into a textbook. Understanding the context for writing critical essays means coming to terms with the *field* of English. (A good place to begin, by the way, is by "eavesdropping" on the profession: the "Preface to the Instructor" that opens this book is important information for you as well.) Put simply, knowledge is power. The more you know about the field's issues, techniques, and motivations, the easier the subject is to learn. Knowing "about" provides "know-how."

How to Use This Book

Writing about Literature is not meant to be the "last word" on how to read and write about literature. It is meant to offer you some first words about how to get more out of your reading and how to write more successful essays.

If you are just starting your formal literary studies, you'll likely want to focus most of your attention on Chapters 1, 2, and 5, on the first half of Chapter 3, and on the model essays in Chapter 4. The introductory chapters emphasize two related areas:

- the importance of bringing your personal experience to the reading of literature
- the importance of experiencing the text fully

If you already have some background in literary studies, or if you wish to learn more about the *values*, *methods*, and *approaches* used by professional critics, you'll want to move on to the second half of Chapter 3. This material was added at the prompting of my own students, especially ones who felt trapped in what they called "the B-rut" (where you can't seem to move beyond "good" writing into the "excellent" or A-level range). I've included strategies, drawn from contemporary critical practice, that will enable you to move from a "textual" response to a "field" response. Step-by-step examples will show you how to make a good or already excellent essay still more insightful. The book also includes an additional chapter, with still more step-by-step examples—this time showing how to write about poetry. Taken together, Chapters 3 and 5 are designed to help you go beyond conventional handbook advice and write "like a literary critic."

Writing about Literature also features a selection of student essays and professional essays on Stephen Crane's story "The Bride Comes to Yellow Sky," first published in 1898. The discussion questions and writing activities should help you use these examples as models for your own work. The book concludes with personal statements by four accomplished critics, and with appendix material on language usage and critical resources. These statements and resources suggest directions for further development of your critical-writing skills.

CHAPTER 1

Getting Started: From Personal Response to Field Stance

Overview

The basic premise of this chapter (and the book as a whole) is that writing is *rhetorical*: that we communicate best when we write (1) with a clear purpose, (2) with knowledge of how to go about achieving that purpose, (3) for a specific audience, and (4) in context. This chapter introduces the four contexts for learning that we'll explore together—the *social*, *institutional*, *textual*, and *field* stances. We'll also look at how understanding those stances will help your critical writing. To help put a human face on our subject, you'll find an interview with a literary scholar, Professor Harold Kolb, Jr., on his life as a literature student, critic, and teacher. The chapter concludes with some practical advice on how to write your first critical paper.

We begin with a review of some key rhetorical concerns.

| 1 |

Writing Is Rhetorical

Rhetoric was first developed in ancient Greece as the art of using language effectively in specific situations. The Greeks found that to communicate effectively we need to define our purpose, know our audience, explore our subject fully (keeping our purpose and audience in mind), and arrange our exploration of the subject in a manner that will affect the reader's attitudes and actions.

The better you understand your purpose, the better your writing will be. This means more than producing a list of facts in response to an assigned task (e.g., "Write an analysis of death imagery in 'The Bride Comes to Yellow Sky'") or asking the teacher what he or she wants. To communicate effectively, you need to write your *self* into the essay: you need to clarify your own purpose. Ask yourself whether you want your essay to:

- express your feelings on a particular subject
- explain the significance of a particular subject
- survey what has already been said on the subject

- persuade your reader to agree with your interpretation or point of view
- change your reader's attitude or correct a general misunderstanding

Documenting Your Personal Response

When writing an essay on literature, you should begin by comparing the work with your own experience. For example, how do you connect personally with a particular story? What does the story mean to you? Think about the ways your *personal experiences* or *beliefs* affect your understanding of the story.

For example, when reading Stephen Crane's "The Bride," you might consider the general awkwardness of the newly married couple. What are your attitudes toward love, romance, and marriage? How do those attitudes compare with the representation of love, romance, and marriage in the story? Have you ever felt out of place in a new social setting? Can you identify with the discomfort felt by any of the major characters? What do you think of the other passengers' responses to the couple?

You could also focus on your knowledge of the Old West. What do you know about the characters and history of this period? How did you learn about the Old West? From books, film, TV? Does this period hold any attraction for you? Does Crane's representation of the Old West match your understanding of this period? Does he tell the kind of story you'd expect to read about the Old West?

The questions you ask yourself will depend on your interests and personal background. The important thing is to find some *personal connection* with the story. One of the best ways to document your personal responses is to keep a *response journal* detailing what and how you read. Unlike a diary, a response journal is a place where you can gather your thoughts and reflections, where you can decide on your purpose. Jot down the sort of questions or observations you might normally write into your class notes or in the margins of the text. Keep the journal entries informal, even fragmentary. Use it as a place to sort out your feelings and intentions regarding what you have read. Some of the questions posed in this chapter should offer you a good place to start. If you write in and reread your journal regularly, you'll likely find many strong topics waiting to be developed.

How to Use Your Personal Response

Once you have documented your responses, turn again to the text and look for places (words, descriptions, scenes, attitudes) that seem to contradict or challenge your expectations and values. Trust your intuition here. *Literature is inherently unsettling*: it often encourages us to see the world and ourselves from a new or different perspective. The process of identifying when and where a story unsettles us is a good first step toward writing the essay.

Can you see any pattern to the way the text challenges your expectations? For example, in "The Bride," at the end of the first paragraph, the word "precipice" strikes many readers as a funny way to talk about landscape passing by a train window. If you have ever ridden on a train, you have probably experienced the kind of optical illusion that the narrator describes, where it looks as if the ground is moving and the train is standing still. But how many of us would describe the horizon as a "precipice"? The word disrupts our expectations. It suggests something treacherous, even deadly.

As we proceed through the story, we begin to see other death-related references, some obvious and some very subtle: we are told that the sheriff's marriage "weigh[s] upon him like a leaden slab"; that he speaks "in a mournful cadence, as one announcing death"; that there's a "chapel-like gloom" over the Weary Gentleman saloon; that an "arch of a tomb" seems to form over the outlaw, Scratchy Wilson; that, when he meets Scratchy in the street, the sheriff's "mouth [seems] to be merely a grave for his tongue." "What," we might well ask, "has all this death imagery got to do with marriage and the Old West?" A question like this can form a strong basis for a critical essay.

Other features of the text disturb some readers. The references to clothes seem, to some, excessive, or at least curious. The couple's fascination with time seems a little incongruous. The many nautical references seem, at first glance, out of place in a cowboy story. The description of the bride as a "drooping, drowning woman" needs explaining—as does her reaction to the gunfight scene, where she is described as "a slave to hideous rites gazing at the apparitional snake." There are many, many more possible *entry points* into the story. They all begin with some negotiation between your personal experience and the representation of experience in the text.

Box 1.1: Field Notes from Critical Theory and Psycholinguistics: "How We Read"

In 1968, critic and theorist Louise Rosenblatt published an important reminder that reading is "A Way of Happening." According to Rosenblatt, literature "makes nothing happen"; literature, she explains, "is not a tool, an instrument for accomplishing some end or purpose or task beyond itself." The reader makes literature "happen by calling it forth from the text": for Rosenblatt (and many other readers), literature must be *experienced*, not just decoded:

> We are directly involved; we are active participants in the "Happening." We are aware of what the symbols [in the text] call forth in us. They point to sensations, objects, images, ideas. These we must pattern out of the material that we bring to the work from our past knowledge of life and language. (340–41)

Rosenblatt's notion of reading as "a happening," a process of "patterning out" meaning, corresponds with contemporary psycholinguistic models of how we read.

Old "bottom-up" models suggested that we find meaning *in the text* by decoding letter by letter, word by word. Today, reading is understood as a "top-down" or "interactive" process. Experienced readers, we've learned, do not sound out each letter of a word like C-A-T. Similarly, when we read a phrase like "Once upon __ _____," we have little difficulty filling in the blanks. Reading thus proceeds by installments of *predictions* against which are tested the actualities of the text.

Kenneth Goodman calls reading a "psycholinguistic guessing game," where readers test hypotheses by guessing what comes next in the text. Reading may be seen as a matter of getting your questions answered, and advanced modes of reading (like literary criticism) are largely a matter of knowing the right questions to ask of the text.

Sources: Louise Rosenblatt. "A Way of Happening" *Educational Record*. Washington: American Council on Education, 1968): 339–46. Print; Kenneth Goodman. "Reading: A Psycholinguistic Guessing Game," *Journal of the Reading Specialist* 6.4 (1967): 126–35. Print.

Becoming a Literacy Researcher

Entering the critical conversation means engaging in some preliminary research. To understand the rhetoric of writing literary criticism, you'll need to take on the role of a detective—or, better yet, a "literacy researcher"—searching out the clues to good writing.

Here we move from documenting your personal response to finding the best means of expressing that response. We move from purpose to *audience* and *context*. This move requires you to investigate how the critical community communicates: its purposes, its forms, its places of publication, its values, etc. The work of rhetoric and composition specialists Richard Beach and Susan Hynds is helpful here. They maintain that there are four stances to be taken when developing new discourse practices:

Stances for Learning a New Discourse

- the "social," where someone like you, new to a discipline, negotiates ideas in collaboration with others
- the "institutional," where you learn to adopt the roles and language norms of academe
- the "textual," where you focus on text features and conventions
- the "field," where you engage and exchange ideas as someone knowledgeable about the conventions of a particular academic discipline

The objective here is to look at the task of writing critical essays from as many angles as possible. Literature and composition professor Russell Hunt says that learning to write essays means learning to "invent the genre" for yourself (227). If you are going to become a critic, you need to find out how things are done. But you need to find out for yourself. You are unlikely to learn by simply following someone else's directions. Like painting by numbers, following a prescribed format produces only marginal results—and it does not guarantee that you can do it all (write or paint) yourself. Learning to write for any field means involving yourself in that field; it means becoming so familiar with the field's ways of thinking and writing

| 5 |

that you begin to (1) use its conventions—its word choice, phrasing, metaphors, formats, etc.—with facility, and then, (2) "invent" a form of critical response that best expresses your interests, experiences, and purposes.

To some extent we all learn through trial and error, but it's probably best to learn with our eyes wide open. Social and institutional learning, where we are immersed in the experience, can sometimes make us feel that in "gaining access" to new discourse conventions and attitudes we must give up old ways of speaking, thinking, and writing. This is normal. College programs are designed to make you evaluate (and re-evaluate) your preconceptions. That does not mean that you need to accept every new idea that comes along; it does mean that learning requires a somewhat open mind. When reading a short story, for example, if an idea or a new way of expressing an idea disturbs your usual way of thinking, you should try not to reject it without analysis. Instead, take note of the differences and then pursue an *informed stance*. Learn the conventions so you can use them for your own purposes.

New Contexts for Reading and Writing

The Social Stance

The social stance involves learning from and with others. The social stance is oral, aural, and gestured: you learn by speaking and listening and observing.

During class discussion, what words, ideas, or phrases are repeated by the instructor?

- What questions are asked? Which seem important?
- Do you notice any specialized vocabulary, any metaphors or unusual turns of phrase?
- Which interpretations seem the most convincing? Why?
- What evidence is used to support positions taken?
- When you receive feedback on your essays, which areas receive the most attention?
- When you compare notes with other students, do you notice any pattern of response in the instructor's comments?

The Institutional Stance

Understanding the institutional stance means gaining insight into the institution's premises, rituals, conventions, and goals. Note: these are complex questions, but ones your instructor can help you understand and answer.

- How would you characterize the kind of language used in your college or university?
- How does the college or university organize knowledge?
- What is the college or university's purpose? Can you discover if that purpose has changed over the years?
- What is your relationship to the college or university? What is your family's relationship to the college or university? Are you, for example, the first member of your family to go to university?
- What are the formal expectations for written work?
- What does it mean to construct and conserve knowledge?
- How does the university divide itself into separate faculties and disciplines?
- What constitutes evidence in the different disciplines?
- Why would different academic disciplines develop different ways of communicating?
- How do different disciplines define "literacy" in their fields?
- What do most disciplines have in common?
- How would you characterize the general attitude or tone expressed by academic writing?
- How do academics use writing to communicate with one another? With students? With the general public?

The Textual Stance

The textual stance focuses on professional genres, on forms of writing studied. In English, the textual focus is especially important: to support or prove an interpretation, critics turn first to the text. Critics tend to use direct quotation rather than paraphrase. When writing about a short story, critics will discuss specific textual features such as setting, imagery, point of view—the so-called "formal elements of prose fiction."

THE ESSAY FORM

- How is the critical essay organized?
- What is the logic of this organization?
- What is its tone? Its purpose?
- How would you characterize the audience for such an essay?
- What is the relationship between student essays and professional essays written in the field?
- What special vocabulary do literary critics use?
- How do critics use quotations as evidence?
- What are the elements of an effective introduction? An effective conclusion?
- How is the evidence documented?

LITERARY FORMS

- What is form or genre? How would you define the form of a short story? A novel? A poem? A play? An essay?
- How many different forms of prose fiction can you identify?
- What parts make up each form?
- How are the parts connected?
- What is meant by pattern in literature?
- What is the form's relationship to its audience? To its historical context?
- How and/or why did such a form develop?

Box 1.2: Field Notes from Composition Studies: The Five-Paragraph Theme

At some point most students have come in contact with the five-paragraph theme: an introduction, with the thesis sentence placed at the end of the first paragraph; the body of three paragraphs, each dealing with a different aspect of the thesis; a conclusion, where you summarize your main points.

This five-paragraph structure remains a staple form of high-school English writing, but it has little currency in college. Why?

First of all, we should note that this kind of "format" does some things very well: it helps organize your thoughts; it provides a predictable structure for both writer and reader; it echoes the basic logic of most academic writing (introduce a position and support that position with evidence); and it is highly efficient—an aid to quick writing.

The downside of the form is that it tends to treat all topics as if they can be slotted into a preconceived format: not all topics can—or should—be divided into three parts. In fact, college audiences prefer a narrower focus, one where you say "more about less." The five-paragraph form also leaves little room for either personal exploration or nuanced discussion.

The word "essay" comes from the French *essai*—a try. Writing is a process of discovery, an opportunity to try out new ideas. Each essay in college English should be an exploration, where your treatment of the subject, not the format, determines its organization.

Instead of learning a format, let your purpose, your subject, your audience, and your developing awareness of field concerns guide the form of your essay. The model essays in Chapter 4 of this book and the critical statements in Chapter 6 offer you some alternative models worth considering.

| 9 |

The Field Stance

Learning the field stance means learning how to *think critically about literature*; it means becoming aware of the models, metaphors, values, and assumptions that inform critical practice. Your instructor can help you answer the following questions.

- Where do English departments come from?
- How is the field of English studies organized? What are its areas of study?
- Are all English programs the same?
- *How* do the demands of graduate school differ from what is required of you as an undergraduate?
- *How* would graduate school training affect the way English professors approach literature?
- *How* do critics define their roles socially, academically, and professionally?
- What differences are there in how English professors teach literature and how they write about literature?
- *What* professional associations represent the field? What are the mandate and purpose of these associations?
- How does English (in particular, literary criticism) define itself in relation to other academic disciplines?
- What specialized language and key metaphors do English instructors use? (Hint: see how often they talk of "meaning" in

spatial terms: about reading "deeply," "closely"; about looking for meaning "in the text"; about "layers of meaning.")
- What values do members of the discipline share? How are those values embedded in the metaphors used?
- What constitutes evidence in English studies?
- What critical methods and approaches do critics use?
- What are the major issues in English studies?

Summary: Why It Is so Important to Become Aware of All Four Stances

It might be tempting to focus simply on the textual stance and let the others slide. In practice, however, some knowledge of each stance proves crucial to effective communication and academic success.

The more you know about your purpose, audience, and context, the better your writing will become. Those writing without knowledge of all four stances are likely to misunderstand either the nature of their task or the nature of the instructor's response. For example, the student who writes only an extended *plot summary* (showing that she understands the material by retelling the story) has misunderstood both task and audience. The institutional stance calls for independent thought and a contribution to existing knowledge on the subject. A plot summary does neither. The social stance calls for a collaborative sharing of views. A plot summary is not helpful there, either. The textual stance calls for some formal written analysis of textual features. The plot summary does little of this. And the field stance calls for a framing of the critical issue and the use of disciplinary language, assumptions, and approaches. The plot summary neither identifies an issue nor reflects normal disciplinary practice.

Think also of the student unsure of how much he or she should quote from the text (or incorporate ideas gleaned from class discussion). After all, if the instructor has already read the story (and likely knows it better than the student), what's the point of reminding her of what she already knows? This confusion involves an over-emphasis on the social stance. Remembering that your role is to contribute to the conversation in the field should help here: the textual and field stances require you to write not for a specific instructor, but for the field. If you write your essay for someone *like* your instructor—someone interested in your topic but who was *not privy* to the class discussion (so you may draw on that somewhat) and who read the story several weeks ago (and can bear certain reminders)—you will find yourself addressing an appropriate audience.

Box 1.3: Field Notes from Linguistics: The Effect of Context on Reading

A change in context often affects the way we comprehend—or fail to comprehend. College presents us with new contexts for reading and writing. Not coming to terms with these new contexts prevents many students from succeeding. That's why knowing how you relate to all four stances is so important.

Consider the following experiment, which demonstrates how context affects comprehension. Most students find the following passage difficult to read and hard to remember after reading:

> The procedure is actually quite simple. First you arrange things into different groups depending on their makeup. Of course, one pile may be sufficient depending on how much there is to do. If you have to go somewhere else due to lack of facilities that is the next step; otherwise you are pretty well set. It is important not to overdo any particular endeavor. That is, it is better to do too few things at once than too many. In the short run this may not seem important, but complications from doing too many can easily arise. A mistake can be expensive as well. The manipulation of the appropriate mechanisms should be self-explanatory, and we need not dwell on it here. At first the whole procedure will seem complicated. Soon, however, it will become just another facet of life. It is difficult to foresee any end to the necessity for this task in the immediate future, but then one can never tell.

Did you find it difficult to understand? Now try again, but this time reading the passage "in context." The missing element is the title, "Washing Clothes." Try this passage out on some friends, first asking them to read it out of context, and then providing the title.

Source: John Bransford and Marcia Johnson, "Consideration of Some Problems of Comprehension," *Visual Information Processing*, ed. William G. Chase (New York: Academic Press, 1973), print.

An Interview with a Literary Critic

Dr. Harold Kolb, Jr. is Professor Emeritus of English and American Studies at the University of Virginia. Recipient of numerous awards for teaching and scholarship, he is a widely published author whose books include *A Handbook for Research in American Literature and American Studies* and *A Field Guide to the Study of American Literature*. His "High Noon at Yellow Sky" is included in the collection of exemplary essays in Chapter 4. As you read the interview, try to apply the four stances advocated by Beach and Hynds: see how Professor Kolb characterizes his life as an English student, critic, and teacher in *social, institutional, textual*, and *field* terms.

Tell us about your undergraduate experience as an English student.

I became an English major in college for two reasons. The first was simply that I liked to read. I had discovered that good literature was full of ideas about history, philosophy, psychology, and other aspects of life one could study in departments with those names, but the ideas were put in better form in novels, plays, and poems. A sociology text might provide some interesting concepts, but you had to beat your way through a verbal thicket to get there. Literature packaged ideas with precision and grace, so that reading it was doubly enjoyable. I also liked the way that an author created a little world that the reader could enter, suspending his or her disbelief, as professors later told me Coleridge had said. The second reason I became an English major was that I wanted to become a better writer, not realizing what a steep, lifelong climb that would be.

Would you say more about becoming a better writer? In particular, could you describe the process you went through in learning to move from literary reading to critical writing?

Moving from reading to writing is not the easy and natural step that some people assume. It is, perhaps, like moving from soccer to basketball: there are some things in common—words in one instance, balls in the other—but in both cases it's a whole new game with a new set of skills.

What does it take to become a writer? Four things, in my opinion: a sense of audience, of whom you are writing for; some instruction, whether by teacher, editor, texts, or models; a lot of practice and revision, as is necessary for any complex skill: something to say, that is, something important for the writer to communicate.

The last point connects with critical writing about literature. For many years literary texts served as topics for beginning writers. Then, about a generation ago, literature fell out of favour in many composition programs, partly because it was thought that the teaching of writing was being scanted for the teaching of literature. Now the pendulum has swung back, for teachers of composition have discovered that writing skills cannot be taught in a vacuum. There is no point in honing a knife unless you are going to cut something. Writers need topics that are significant, interesting, profound, enjoyable, disturbing; and that is precisely what literary texts provide.

When you were an undergraduate, was there a particular piece of advice or an insight that helped you develop as a writer?

No and yes. I did my undergraduate work at Amherst College in Massachusetts, where the faculty assumed, naively of course, that writing ability was a prerequisite for college work. Consequently, there was no freshman composition class, no course in advanced writing, no explicit writing instruction of any kind. There was, however, something even more important—an unstated belief, impalpable and ever present as the Connecticut Valley air, that an educated person should be a competent writer. Even my first-year roommate, a football player, wanted to learn how to write, and I taught myself a good deal while trying to tutor him. I also learned from occasional remarks by instructors on papers, hints about writing skills sandwiched between long comments on content ("wrong connotation," "this section doesn't seem to fit here," "why are these paragraphs so short?"), even though I was left to figure out solutions for myself. And most of all I learned from constant practice. Writing, the faculty realized, was the most active form of learning. Some courses required weekly papers and virtually every course, even those in the sciences, based much of its pedagogy on written assignments. Many students completed their undergraduate days, as I did, by producing a 65-page senior thesis.

I thought, of course, I had left this writing regimen behind when, sprung loose from college, I entered my first career—that of a US Navy pilot. Thus I was astonished to hear the commanding officer of my first squadron lecture newcomers about the importance of the written work expected of all officers. "Incompetent pilots don't come back," he said. "Incompetent writers don't get promoted."

Not all critics and teachers agree on the best way to approach writing about literature, and, especially within the last two decades, there's been much discussion about ways to contextualize, enhance, and/or challenge traditional "close-reading" techniques. What are the current critical approaches? And what are the implications for writing about literature?

| 14 |

In the late nineteenth century, when English departments were relatively new in North American colleges and universities, teachers of literature tended to lecture on the biographies of authors. Today the reigning school of criticism concerns the politics of cultural identity. The intervening decades have seen a dozen or more theories of literary criticism rise to prominence: historical, social, formalist and New Critical, textual, generic, psychological, Marxist, structuralist, reader response, feminist, deconstructionist. One way to make sense of this variety of intellectual options is to see them not as competing ideologies, but rather as multiple contributions, a kind of tool kit, for the complex task of unlocking the richness of literary art.

In addition to this variety of critical approaches, literary study also presents the student with a variety of components for study. These include the sources and background of a work; the author's life, letters, and journals; properties of the text such as narrative strategy, characterization, and style; circumstances of publication and reception; and the interpretation of the work in its time and

our own. In order to determine which critical tools to use, which components to focus on, a person who writes on a literary topic has to answer three questions: What particular strengths (in my personal history, knowledge, other reading, interests, values) do I bring to the task? What thesis is most likely to illuminate the significance of the work? What critical approach and what focus make most sense in attempting to prove my thesis about the work? If the topic is *King Lear*, one might need to consider the psychological dynamics of the family. If a writer is quoting Hamlet's famous line, as printed in the 1623 folio text, "O that this too too solid flesh would melt," he or she needs to be aware that the 1604–05 quarto text reads "sallied," and that Hamlet may well mean "sullied" rather than "solid." If the discussion concerns Stephen Crane and the Western, the writer needs to know something about the real history of the American West and the false history portrayed in popular literature.

Can you illustrate for us how a student might go about distinguishing between real and false histories? Where does one begin?

I begin with the assumption that most histories are both real and false. That is, as John DeForest, Union company commander and Civil War novelist, put it in *Miss Ravenel's Conversion from Secession to Loyalty*, "I suppose that only Deity sees [the world] truly." The words "history" and "story" have the same etymological parent, Latin *historia*. History, then, is someone's story of the past—"the memory," according to Carl Becker, "of things said and done." It is "the memory" of human beings, and humans necessarily have limited and partial points of view. The "things said and done" that are remembered and written down are only a tiny fragment of the huge rolling panorama of the past. Thus we have a multitude of differing historical opinions. In 1883, Frank Leslie's *Illustrated Weekly* described cowboys as "foul-mouthed, drunken, lecherous, and utterly corrupt." Five years later, Theodore Roosevelt opined that they possessed "to a very high degree the stern, manly qualities which are important to a nation."

Some histories are more real than others, and a key task for the student is to learn the difference. I like primary sources, first-hand observations, specifics, facts, measurements. Farmers rushed west of the 100th meridian because speculators like Charles Wilber told them that "rain follows the plough." If they had stopped to consult J.W. Powell's *Report on the Lands of the Arid Region*, they wouldn't have been so surprised to see their crops fail. When I pick up a history book or article I want to know who the author is, what his or her credentials are, what biases might be present, to what extent differing opinions are represented. I look at the date, for I prefer the earliest account

(that closest to the event) and the most recent intervening histories. I look to see if the publisher is reputable, if the text is carefully edited, and if the author has provided footnotes or endnotes, a bibliography, and an index. A good scholar leaves a trail that readers can ride for themselves.

I'd like to hear more about your own critical approach and how you've employed it in your "The Bride Comes to Yellow Sky" essay. Historical research, as you've described it, seems important— but I'm wondering what other methods you used in putting the essay together.

As a literary critic I believe in pluralism, pragmatism, and opportunism, using that last word in the positive way that Henry Nash Smith intended when he described his theory of American Studies as "principled opportunism." That is, I define the task I am trying to accomplish and then figure out what critical approach or approaches are likely to prove most fruitful. Part of the method of "High Noon at Yellow Sky" is derived from the approach Smith developed in his *Virgin Land*, one of the first books to reach beyond high-brow/low-brow classifications and demonstrate the significance of popular literature in defining the aspirations, fears, and dreams of the public that consumes it. The usefulness, and the danger, of popular culture is that it tells us what we already believe. While there is often no clear-cut distinction between popular forms and those we would

| 15 |

classify as great art, the latter tend to complicate, put pressure on, transcend what Canadian psycholinguist Frank Smith calls "the theory of the world in our heads."

The other major approach in the article is generic and formalist—my attempt to describe the nature and the possibilities of parody. Now that you make me step back and think about it, I see that these two approaches—cultural and formalist— often thought of as opposed, seem appropriate together since the article is located at the intersection of the popular appeal represented by *High Noon* and the more subtle artistic genius of Stephen Crane.

When you say that popular culture tends to reinforce what we already believe, I assume that you are suggesting a very different role for literature—that, unlike popular culture, it challenges our beliefs. It seems to me that university English classes do something similar: they challenge us to read and write differently. I'm wondering what common challenges your students encounter when they first start studying literature. Do they have any common misconceptions about "English"?

That's a tough question, since I'm reluctant to speak for my students and since they have different kinds of challenges. I have, however, seen one particular challenge often enough to risk a generalization. Although they express the point in various ways, a number of students seem

discouraged, sometimes dismayed, by the fact that the bar has been raised between high school and college. "I learned how to read stories and write about them in high school," one disconsolate advisee told me. "I was really good at it and got A's. Now my instructor, who just gave me a C, tells me that what I learned will make 'a good platform' for understanding literature better and writing about it more persuasively."

My response to this student was that he and his classmates should be grateful, for they are learning that they selected a good college—one that will take them beyond what they now know, what they can now do. But it's a tough lesson. I remember graduating from officers' candidate school, and thinking, for about 24 hours, that as a newly minted commissioned officer, I finally had it made. Then I discovered that, as one of the most junior officers in the entire navy, I was fair game for the worst assignments and the fewest privileges. It turns out that if you are successful in climbing up a ladder, what you reach is the bottom of the next ladder.

Do you have any final words of advice for a student writing his or her first critical paper on a story like "The Bride Comes to Yellow Sky"?

That question comes across like a fat pitch to any English teacher; the danger is that I'll attempt to hit it out of the park with a 10,000-word answer.

Let me try briefly to walk a student through the writing process as I have come to know it through years of writing and teaching.

First comes *reading*. Forget classes, assignments, literary criticism, editors' introductions, and possible topics. Get comfortable, put your feet up, and let yourself down into the world of the story. Experience it. Enjoy it. Then take a break. Let the narrative and its characters swirl around in your unconscious mind while you go for a walk, shoot a few baskets, or have a cappuccino with a friend.

Then *reread* the story, this time engaging your intellect to buttress your emotions by looking for the ways in which the author led you to the effect the story had on you. You might jot down things that were of interest to you, questions you had, ways in which the narrative connected to what you have already read or experienced, ways in which the narrative surprised you, taught you something new. Organize these miscellaneous notes into groups with common denominators, such as the point of view of the tale, the author, the historical context, or the style. Choose one of these groups to pursue, and you will have what I call an *area*.

Learn more about that area by looking again at the text and doing some research if necessary. Ask yourself the questions mentioned earlier about which critical approaches to use, which literary components to focus on in illuminating the significance of the work. If the story is "The Open Boat" and you are interested in the author, you will need to find out that Stephen Crane, as a 25-year-old reporter, shipped aboard a munitions boat headed for Cuba on 1 January 1897, that the boat sank about 15 miles off Daytona Beach, and that, after spending the night in a 10-foot dinghy with three other men, Crane and his companions were swamped in the surf when they came ashore at dawn on January 3rd. Let's say that, in discovering these details, you also find out that Crane wrote an account of the experience right after it happened for the *New York Press*, and that the Press story differs from "The Open Boat," which was written later. Eureka! You have discovered a good topic inside your area—the differences between the newspaper report of Crane's experience and the story.

But wait a minute, you are not ready to write yet. You have completed only two of three preliminary steps. The crucial third step is to decide what it is that you are going to say about those differences, what you are trying to prove, what, in short, your *thesis* is. You might, for example, want to demonstrate how the creative writer selects from the raw materials of experience. The story concerns only part of the historical events, even though it is four times longer than the newspaper report. You might want to demonstrate how some statements in the news account ("there was an enormous sea running") are enhanced in the tale ("these waves were most wrongfully and barbarously abrupt and tall"); you might want to show how the story transcends news accounts by moving from fact to interpreted experience, leaving readers, like the men in the open boat, feeling "that they could then be interpreters." There are many other possibilities, and you can't do justice to them all. Pick one and stick to it. The thesis of a critical essay is what the plot is to a story: it holds everything together.

Now you are ready to write a *rough draft*, which, for me, is a rapid, exploratory statement of the main ideas, without worrying about the sequence of the materials, repetitions, contradictions, grammar, spelling, or polish. The purpose of the rough draft is to get your ideas out where you can see them, to discover if your thesis is going to hold up. Then take a recess, or a shower, or go to bed—give your unconscious mind a chance to cut in and sort things out. After this interval, review the rough draft (perhaps with your instructor). There are three possibilities at this point: your thesis is not going to work and you need to return to the topic stage; your thesis is basically sound, but needs some adjustments; your thesis is solid and you can sail on to the *second draft*.

The second draft should be a total rewriting of the rough draft, not simply a Band-Aid job. Start with a clean computer screen, with the rough draft pushed down (or printed out) so you can refer to it but not be

trapped by it. In the second draft you should put the large units of structure in place, devise the best order of paragraphs and blocks of paragraphs, check for logical connections, select appropriate evidence, and prune the exuberances and exaggerations of the rough draft. Often the second draft will be shorter than the rough draft.

For the *third draft*, the one you are going to hand in, you need to work on the smaller details, which normally can be done as a revision, on screen, of the second draft. This is the time to devise an effective opening and conclusion, weed out writer-based prose (which the writer but not the reader can understand), and tune for precise phrasing, appropriate sentence rhythm and variety, and clear transitions between paragraphs.

You are almost finished. All you have left is the *clean-up*, which has two parts. First check facts, dates, names, quotations, citations, footnotes, spelling, grammar, punctuation. Then proofread, twice: once quickly, for sense; once slowly, for typography.

The two most important points in this process are making sure that you push yourself to create a thesis inside the too-wide world of the topic, and that you rewrite rather than merely correct the rough draft. Both of these points involve *revision*, and when I first learned that, I thought I had really discovered something. "Hey, writing is revision," I used to tell my students and my colleagues. That is certainly true, but what I gradually came to realize is that history is revision, architecture is revision, geology is revision. Revision is the way the mind works, testing and modifying and retesting. The very molecules in our bodies—about 7 per cent each day—are taken apart and reassembled. Revision is such a powerful aspect of writing because everything, life itself, is revision.

Exercises

Social and Institutional Stances

1. Using the Kolb interview as a model, pose the same (or similar) questions to a literature instructor at your own college or university. Compare the responses. Are their backgrounds and attitudes similar? Do they seem to hold the same values? Why do they believe that writing about literature is an important activity? Prepare an oral report for the class.

2. Ask a student in your class some of the same questions. How do his or her responses differ from the professors' responses? Present your findings to the class.

3. Read through your college's calendar and compare two or three program descriptions. What purposes and values are highlighted? How do these purposes and values differ? Write a paragraph where you reflect on the "institutional" face of English studies represented in your college calendar.

Textual Stance

1. Keep a journal where you document your own responses to (a) classroom discussions; (b) key words, metaphors, and technical terms used in your literature class or that you have found in your outside reading; (c) the literary works as you read them. Try to maintain daily entries and review them at least every other week.

2. Read carefully one of the sample essays from Chapter 4. Identify the essay's purpose, its intended audience, its tone, its organizational structure, and any textual conventions that seem out of the ordinary. On the basis of your observations, write a 200-word recipe for writing "the critical essay" (e.g., "First add the author's name, the title of the story, and a comment on the story's theme …").

Field Stance

1. Go to the library and find the names of several contemporary critics who have written about "The Bride Comes to Yellow Sky" or any other work on your course's reading list. Read through the critic's writing and, in your journal, write a brief response where you either confirm or take issue with the critic's position.

2. Join an online literature discussion list, blog, or other forum (see the "Resources" section of this book for some electronic addresses) and, after "eavesdropping" for a week or two, post a brief note or entry. You can try asking a question—or, better yet, try contributing to the discussion thread. In your journal describe the experience and explain how you decided on the voice, language, and message that would fit the "electronic discourse."

CHAPTER 2

Reading and Responding to Stephen Crane's "The Bride Comes to Yellow Sky"

Overview

In this chapter you'll read Stephen Crane's short story "The Bride Comes to Yellow Sky," as it first appeared with illustrations in *McClure's Magazine*. You'll also read Eric Gislason's review of critical response to the story. This chapter asks you to interact with both the story and the critical responses. Read actively. Ask questions of the text.

Read the story carefully, with pen or pencil in hand. In the margin, jot down your thoughts on aspects of the text that challenge your expectations. Also note key words and patterns—or references that interest you. Try to identify as many patterns and as many issues as possible. Once you have finished reading the story, discuss it with others in your class. Compare notes and form your own response to the story *before* proceeding on to Gislason's literature review of critical responses.

In an October 1897 letter to his American literary agent, Paul Revere Reynolds, Stephen Crane wrote: "'The Bride Comes to Yellow Sky' is a daisy and don't let them talk funny about it" (qtd. in LaFrance 214). In February 1898, *McClure's Magazine* published the story, and for over a hundred years readers and critics have talked about it in all kinds of ways. "The Bride" has been widely read and interpreted, and today it is firmly established as an important work in the canon of contemporary prose fiction.

THE BRIDE COMES TO YELLOW SKY.

by Stephen Crane

Author of "The Red Badge of Courage," "The Third Violet," etc.

I.

THE great Pullman was whirling onward with such dignity of motion that a glance from the window seemed simply to prove that the plains of Texas were pouring eastward. Vast flats of green grass, dull-hued spaces of mesquite and cactus, little groups of frame houses, woods of light and tender trees, all were sweeping into the east, sweeping over the horizon, a precipice.

A newly married pair had boarded this coach at San Antonio. The man's face was reddened from many days in the wind and sun, and a direct result of his new black clothes was that his brick-colored hands were constantly performing in a most conscious fashion. From time to time he looked down respectfully at his attire. He sat with a hand on each knee, like a man waiting in a barber's shop. The glances he devoted to other passengers were furtive and shy.

The bride was not pretty, nor was she very young. She wore a dress of blue cashmere, with small reservations of velvet here and there and with steel buttons abounding. She continually twisted her head to regard her puff sleeves, very stiff, straight, and high. They embarrassed her. It was quite apparent that she had cooked, and that she expected to cook, dutifully. The blushes caused by the careless scrutiny of some passengers as she had entered the car were strange to see upon this plain, under-class countenance, which was drawn in placid, almost emotionless lines.

They were evidently very happy. "Ever been in a parlor-car before?" he asked, smiling with delight.

"No," she answered. "I never was. It's fine, ain't it?"

"Great! And then after a while we'll go forward to the diner and get a big layout. Finest meal in the world. Charge a dollar."

"Oh, do they?" cried the bride. "Charge a dollar? Why, that's too much —for us—ain't it, Jack?"

"Not this trip, anyhow," he answered bravely. "We're going to go the whole thing."

Later, he explained to her about the trains. "You see, it's a thousand miles from one end of Texas to the other, and this train runs right across it and never stops but four times." He had the pride of an owner. He pointed out to her the dazzling fittings of the coach, and in truth her eyes opened wider as she contemplated the sea-green figured velvet, the shining brass, silver, and glass, the wood that gleamed as darkly brilliant as the surface of a pool of oil. At one end a bronze figure sturdily held a support for a separated chamber, and at convenient places on the ceiling were frescoes in olive and silver.

To the minds of the pair, their surroundings reflected the glory of their marriage that morning in San Antonio. This was the environment of their new estate, and the man's face in particular beamed with an elation that made him appear ridiculous to the negro porter. This individual at times surveyed them from afar with an amused and superior grin. On other occasions he bullied them with skill in ways that did not make it exactly plain to them that they were being bullied. He subtly used all the manners of the most

377

THE BRIDE COMES TO YELLOW SKY.

unconquerable kind of snobbery. He oppressed them, but of this oppression they had small knowledge, and they speedily forgot that infrequently a number of travelers covered them with stares of derisive enjoyment. Historically there was supposed to be something infinitely humorous in their situation.

"We are due in Yellow Sky at 3.42," he said, looking tenderly into her eyes.

"Oh, are we?" she said, as if she had not been aware of it. To evince surprise at her husband's statement was part of her wifely amiability. She took from a pocket a little silver watch, and as she held it before her and stared at it with a frown of attention, the new husband's face shone.

"I bought it in San Anton' from a friend of mine," he told her gleefully.

"It's seventeen minutes past twelve," she said, looking up at him with a kind of shy and clumsy coquetry. A passenger, noting this play, grew excessively sardonic, and winked at himself in one of the numerous mirrors.

At last they went to the dining-car. Two rows of negro waiters, in glowing white suits, surveyed their entrance with the interest and also the equanimity of men who had been forewarned. The pair fell to the lot of a waiter who happened to feel pleasure in steering them through their meal. He viewed them with the manner of a fatherly pilot, his countenance radiant with benevolence. The patronage, entwined with the ordinary deference, was not plain to them. And yet, as they returned to their coach, they showed in their faces a sense of escape.

To the left, miles down a long purple slope, was a little ribbon of mist where moved the keening Rio Grande. The train was approaching it at an angle, and the apex was Yellow Sky. Presently it was apparent that, as the distance from Yellow Sky grew shorter, the husband became commensurately restless. His brick-red hands were more insistent in their prominence. Occasionally he was even rather absent-minded and far-away when the bride leaned forward and addressed him.

As a matter of truth, Jack Potter was beginning to find the shadow of a deed weigh upon him like a leaden slab. He, the town marshal of Yellow Sky, a man known, liked, and feared in his corner, a prominent person, had gone to San Antonio to meet a girl he believed he loved, and there, after the usual prayers, had actually induced her to marry him, without consulting Yellow Sky for any part of the transaction. He was now bringing his bride before an innocent and unsuspecting community.

Of course, people in Yellow Sky married as it pleased them in accordance with a general custom; but such was Potter's thought of his duty to his friends, or of their idea of his duty, or of an unspoken form which does not control men in these matters, that he felt he was heinous. He had committed an extraordinary crime. Face to face with this girl in San Antonio, and spurred by his sharp impulse, he had gone headlong over all the social hedges. At San Antonio he was like a man hidden in the dark. A knife to sever any friendly duty, any form, was easy to his hand in that remote city. But the hour of Yellow Sky, the hour of daylight, was approaching.

He knew full well that his marriage was an important thing to his town. It could only be exceeded by the burning of the new hotel. His friends could not forgive him. Frequently he had reflected on the advisability of telling them by telegraph, but a new cowardice had been upon him.

"He sat with a hand on each knee, like a man waiting in a barber's shop"

24

"—and at the moment that the old man fell down stairs with the bureau in his arms, the old woman was coming up with two scuttles of coal, and, of course—"

He feared to do it. And now the train was hurrying him toward a scene of amazement, glee, reproach. He glanced out of the window at the line of haze swinging slowly in toward the train.

Yellow Sky had a kind of brass band, which played painfully, to the delight of the populace. He laughed without heart as he thought of it. If the citizens could dream with his prospective arrival with his bride, they would parade the band at the station and escort them, amid cheers and laughing congratulations, to his adobe home.

He resolved that he would use all the devices of speed and plains-craft in making the journey from the station to his house. Once within that safe citadel, he could issue some sort of a vocal bulletin, and then not go among the citizens until they had time to wear off a little of their enthusiasm.

The bride looked anxiously at him. "What's worrying you, Jack?"

He laughed again. "I'm not worrying, girl. I'm only thinking of Yellow Sky."

She flushed in comprehension.

A sense of mutual guilt invaded their minds and developed a finer tenderness. They looked at each other with eyes softly aglow. But Potter often laughed the same nervous laugh. The flush upon the bride's face seemed quite permanent.

The traitor to the feelings of Yellow Sky narrowly watched the speeding landscape. "We're nearly there," he said.

Presently the porter came and announced the proximity of Potter's home. He held a brush in his hand and, with all his airy superiority gone, he brushed Potter's new clothes as the latter slowly turned this way and that way. Potter fumbled out a coin and gave it to the porter, as he had seen others do. It was a heavy and muscle-bound business, as that of a man shoeing his first horse.

The porter took their bag, and as the train began to slow they moved forward to the hooded platform of the car. Presently the two engines and their long string of coaches rushed into the station of Yellow Sky.

"They have to take water here," said Potter, from a constricted throat and in mournful cadence, as one announcing death. Before the train stopped, his eye had swept the length of the platform, and he was glad and astonished to see there was none upon it but the station-agent, who, with a slightly hurried and anxious air, was walking toward the water-tanks. When the train had halted, the porter

THE BRIDE COMES TO YELLOW SKY.

alighted first and placed in position a little temporary step.

"Come on, girl," said Potter hoarsely. As he helped her down they each laughed on a false note. He took the bag from the negro, and bade his wife cling to his arm. As they slunk rapidly away, his hang-dog glance perceived that they were unloading the two trunks, and also that the station-agent far ahead near the baggage-car had turned and was running toward him, making gestures. He laughed, and groaned as he laughed, when he noted the first effect of his marital bliss upon Yellow Sky. He gripped his wife's arm firmly to his side, and they fled. Behind them the porter stood chuckling fatuously.

Jack Potter

II.

The California Express on the Southern Railway was due at Yellow Sky in twenty-one minutes. There were six men at the bar of the "Weary Gentleman" saloon. One was a drummer who talked a great deal and rapidly; three were Texans who did not care to talk at that time; and two were Mexican sheep-herders who did not talk as a general practice in the "Weary Gentleman" saloon. The barkeeper's dog lay on the board walk that crossed in front of the door. His head was on his paws, and he glanced drowsily here and there with the constant vigilance of a dog that is kicked on occasion. Across the sandy street were some vivid green grass plots, so wonderful in appearance amid the sands that burned near them in a blazing sun that they caused a doubt in the mind. They exactly resembled the grass mats used to represent lawns on the stage. At the cooler end of the railway station a man without a coat sat in a tilted chair and smoked his pipe. The fresh-cut bank of the Rio Grande circled near the town, and there could be seen beyond it a great, plum-colored plain of mesquite.

Save for the busy drummer and his

Scratchy Wilson

companions in the saloon, Yellow Sky was dozing. The new-comer leaned gracefully upon the bar, and recited many tales with the confidence of a bard who has come upon a new field.

"—and at the moment that the old man fell down stairs with the bureau in his arms, the old woman was coming up with two scuttles of coal, and, of course—"

The drummer's tale was interrupted by a young man who suddenly appeared in the open door. He cried: "Scratchy Wilson's drunk, and has turned loose with both hands." The two Mexicans at once set down their glasses and faded out of the rear entrance of the saloon.

The drummer, innocent and jocular, answered: "All right, old man. S'pose he has. Come in and have a drink, anyhow."

But the information had made such an obvious cleft in every skull in the room that the drummer was obliged to see its importance. All had become instantly solemn. "Say," said he, mystified, "what is this?" His three companions made the introductory gesture of eloquent speech, but the young man at the door forestalled them.

"It means, my friend," he answered, as he came into the saloon, "that for the next two hours this town won't be a health resort."

The barkeeper went to the door and locked and barred it. Reaching out of the window, he pulled in heavy wooden shutters and barred them. Immediately a solemn, chapel-like gloom was upon the place. The drummer was looking from one to another.

"But say," he cried, "what is this, anyhow? You don't mean there is going to be a gun-fight?"

"Don't know whether there'll be a fight or not," answered one man grimly. "But there'll be some shootin'—some good shootin'."

The young man who had warned them waved his hand. "Oh, there'll be a fight fast enough, if anyone wants it. Anybody can get a fight out there in the street. There's a fight just waiting."

The drummer seemed to be swayed between the interest of a foreigner and a perception of personal danger.

"What did you say his name was?" he asked.

"Scratchy Wilson," they answered in chorus.

"And will he kill anybody? What are you going to do? Does this happen often? Does he rampage around like this out and fights Scratchy when he gets on one of these tears."

"Wow," said the drummer, mopping his brow. "Nice job he's got."

The voices had toned away to mere whisperings. The drummer wished to ask further questions which were born of an increasing anxiety and bewilderment; but when he attempted them, the men merely looked at him in irritation and motioned him to remain silent. A tense waiting hush was upon them. In the deep shad-

The man yelled, and the dog broke into a gallop."

once a week or so? Can he break in that door?"

"No, he can't break down that door," replied the barkeeper. "He's tried it three times. But when he comes you'd better lay down on the floor, stranger. He's dead sure to shoot at it, and a bullet may come through."

Thereafter the drummer kept a strict eye upon the door. The time had not yet been called for him to hug the floor, but, as a minor precaution, he sidled near to the wall. "Will he kill anybody?" he said again.

The men laughed low and scornfully at the question.

"He's out to shoot, and he's out for trouble. Don't see any good in experimentin' with him."

"But what do you do in a case like this? What do you do?"

A man responded: "Why, he and Jack Potter—"

But, in chorus, the other men interrupted. "Jack Potter's in San Anton'."

"Well, who is he? What's he got to do with it?"

"Oh, he's the town marshal. He goes ows of the room their eyes shone as they listened for sounds from the street. One man made three gestures at the barkeeper, and the latter, moving like a ghost, handed him a glass and a bottle. The man poured a full glass of whisky, and set down the bottle noiselessly. He gulped the whisky in a swallow, and turned again toward the door in immovable silence. The drummer saw that the barkeeper, without a sound, had taken a Winchester from beneath the bar. Later he saw this individual beckoning to him, so he tiptoed across the room.

"You better come with me back of the bar."

"No, thanks," said the drummer, perspiring. "I'd rather be where I can make a break for the back door."

Whereupon the man of bottles made a kindly but peremptory gesture. The drummer obeyed it, and finding himself seated on a box with his head below the level of the bar, balm was laid upon his soul at sight of various zinc and copper fittings that bore a resemblance to armorplate. The barkeeper took a seat comfortably upon an adjacent box.

"You see," he whispered, "this here Scratchy Wilson is a wonder with a gun— a perfect wonder—and when he goes on the war trail, we hunt our holes—naturally. He's about the last one of the old gang that used to hang out along the river here. He's a terror when he's drunk. When he's sober he's all right—kind of simple— wouldn't hurt a fly—nicest fellow in town. But when he's drunk—whoo!"

There were periods of stillness. "I wish Jack Potter was back from San Anton'," said the barkeeper. "He shot Wilson up once—in the leg—and he would sail in and pull out the kinks in this thing."

Presently they heard from a distance the sound of a shot, followed by three wild yowls. It instantly removed a bond from the men in the darkened saloon. There was a shuffling of feet. They looked at each other. "Here he comes," they said.

III.

A man in a maroon-colored flannel shirt, which had been purchased for purposes of decoration and made, principally, by some Jewish women on the east side of New York, rounded a corner and walked into the middle of the main street of Yellow Sky. In either hand the man held a long, heavy, blue-black revolver. Often he yelled, and these cries rang through a semblance of a deserted village, shrilly flying over the roofs in a volume that seemed to have no relation to the ordinary vocal strength of a man. It was as if the surrounding stillness formed the arch of a tomb over him. These cries of ferocious challenge rang against walls of silence. And his boots had red tops with gilded imprints, of the kind beloved in winter by little sledding boys on the hillsides of New England.

The man's face flamed in a rage begot of whisky. His eyes, rolling and yet keen for ambush, hunted the still doorways and windows. He walked with the creeping movement of the midnight cat. As it occurred to him, he roared menacing information. The long revolvers in his hands were as easy as straws; they were moved with an electric swiftness. The little fingers of each hand played sometimes in a musician's way. Plain from the low collar of the shirt, the cords of his neck straightened and sank, straightened and sank, as passion moved him. The only sounds were his terrible invitations. The calm adobes preserved their demeanor

at the passing of this small thing in the middle of the street.

There was no offer of fight; no offer of fight. The man called to the sky. There were no attractions. He bellowed and fumed and swayed his revolvers here and everywhere.

The dog of the barkeeper of the "Weary Gentleman" saloon had not appreciated the advance of events. He yet lay dozing in front of his master's door. At sight of the dog, the man paused and raised his revolver humorously. At sight of the man, the dog sprang up and walked diagonally away, with a sullen head, and growling. The man yelled, and the dog broke into a gallop. As it was about to enter an alley, there was a loud noise, a whistling, and something spat the ground directly before it. The dog screamed, and, wheeling in terror, galloped headlong in a new direction. Again there was a noise, a whistling, and sand was kicked viciously before it. Fear-stricken, the dog turned and flurried like an animal in a pen. The man stood laughing, his weapons at his hips.

Ultimately the man was attracted by the closed door of the "Weary Gentleman" saloon. He went to it, and hammering with a revolver, demanded drink.

The door remaining imperturbable, he picked a bit of paper from the walk and nailed it to the framework with a knife. He then turned his back contemptuously upon this popular resort, and walking to the opposite side of the street, and spinning there on his heel quickly and lithely, fired at the bit of paper. He missed it by a half inch. He swore at himself, and went away. Later, he comfortably fusilladed the windows of his most intimate friend. The man was playing with this town. It was a toy for him.

But still there was no offer of fight. The name of Jack Potter, his ancient antagonist, entered his mind, and he concluded that it would be a glad thing if he should go to Potter's house and by bombardment induce him to come out and fight. He moved in the direction of his desire, chanting Apache scalp-music.

When he arrived at it, Potter's house presented the same still front as had the other adobes. Taking up a strategic position, the man howled a challenge. But this house regarded him as might a great stone god. It gave no sign. After a decent wait, the man howled further challenges, mingling with them wonderful epithets.

Presently there came the spectacle of a man churning himself into deepest rage over the immobility of a house. He fumed at it as the winter wind attacks a prairie cabin in the North. To the distance there should have gone the sound of a tumult like the fighting of 200 Mexi-

I ain't got a gun on me, Scratchy, ... Honest, I ain't."

cans. As necessity bade him, he paused for breath or to reload his revolvers.

IV.

Potter and his bride walked sheepishly and with speed. Sometimes they laughed together shamefacedly and low.

"Next corner, dear," he said finally.

They put forth the efforts of a pair walking bowed against a strong wind. Potter was about to raise a finger to point the first appearance of the new home when, as they circled the corner, they came face to face with a man in a maroon-colored shirt who was feverishly pushing cartridges into a large revolver. Upon the instant the man dropped this revolver to the ground, and, like lightning, whipped

another from its holster. The second weapon was aimed at the bridegroom's chest.

There was a silence. Potter's mouth seemed to be merely a grave for his tongue. He exhibited an instinct to at once loosen his arm from the woman's grip, and he dropped the bag to the sand. As for the bride, her face had gone as yellow as old cloth. She was a slave to hideous rites gazing at the apparitional snake.

The two men faced each other at a distance of three paces. He of the revolver smiled with a new and quiet ferocity. "Tried to sneak up on me," he said. "Tried to sneak up on me!" His eyes grew more baleful. As Potter made a slight movement, the man thrust his revolver venomously forward. "No, don't you do it, Jack Potter. Don't you move a finger toward a gun just yet. Don't you move an eyelash. The time has come for me to settle with you, and I'm goin' to do it my own way and loaf along with no interferin'. So if you don't want a gun bent on you, just mind what I tell you."

Potter looked at his enemy. "I ain't got a gun on me, Scratchy," he said. "Honest, I ain't." He was stiffening and steadying, but yet somewhere at the back of his mind a vision of the Pullman floated, the sea-green figured velvet, the shining brass, silver, and glass, the wood that gleamed as darkly brilliant as the surface of a pool of oil—all the glory of the marriage, the environment of the new estate. "You know I fight when it comes to fighting, Scratchy Wilson, but I ain't got a gun on me. You'll have to do all the shootin' yourself."

THE BRIDE COMES TO YELLOW SKY.

His enemy's face went livid. He stepped forward and lashed his weapon to and fro before Potter's chest. "Don't you tell me you ain't got no gun on you, you whelp. Don't tell me no lie like that. There ain't a man in Texas ever seen you without no gun. Don't take me for no kid." His eyes blazed with light, and his throat worked like a pump.

"I ain't takin' you for no kid," answered Potter. His heels had not moved an inch backward. "I'm takin' you for a — fool. I tell you I ain't got a gun, and I ain't. If you're goin' to shoot me up, you better begin now. You'll never get a chance like this again."

So much enforced reasoning had told on Wilson's rage. He was calmer. "If you ain't got a gun, why ain't you got a gun?" he sneered. "Been to Sunday-school?"

"I ain't got a gun because I've just come from San Anton' with my wife. I'm married," said Potter. "And if I'd thought there was going to be any ga-loots like you prowling around when I brought my wife home, I'd had a gun, and don't you forget it."

"Married!" said Scratchy, not at all comprehending.

"Yes, married. I'm married," said Potter distinctly.

"Married?" said Scratchy. Seemingly for the first time he saw the drooping, drowning woman at the other man's side. "No!" he said. He was like a creature allowed a glimpse of another world. He moved a pace backward, and his arm with the revolver dropped to his side. "Is this the lady?" he asked.

"Yes, this is the lady," answered Potter.

There was another period of silence.

"Well," said Wilson at last, slowly, "I s'pose it's all off now."

"It's all off if you say so, Scratchy. You know I didn't make the trouble." Potter lifted his valise.

"Well, I 'low it's off, Jack," said Wilson. He was looking at the ground. "Married!" He was not a student of chivalry; it was merely that in the presence of this foreign condition he was a simple child of the earlier plains. He picked up his starboard revolver, and placing both weapons in their holsters, he went away. His feet made funnel-shaped tracks in the heavy sand.

29

"Married!"

Response Notes

At this point you should collect your thoughts and margin notes. Mark any elements repeated in the text (patterns). Mark any passages that seem unclear, curious, or disturbing. Re-scan the story, this time noting how the marked patterns and passages relate to such elements as imagery, setting, point of view, characterization, plot structure, narrative voice, mood, and prose style. Ask yourself what effect these formal elements have on your reading.

Also consider the images that accompanied the 1898 printing. The illustrations by Ernest L. Blumenschein are a form of interpretation, too. Does the illustrator's version of the story match the images you create in your mind's eye? How would you illustrate the story?

The Critical Conversation

An important way to approach "The Bride"—indeed, any work of prose fiction—is by entering the critical conversation of readings already documented. If you've begun to discuss the story with others in your class, you have adopted the *social stance* toward learning critical discourse. This is an important first step. If you've marked up the text, paying particular attention to the literary patterns, you have taken on a *textual stance*. The *institutional stance* depends on the level of formality and academic rigour you've used to prepare your notes. The *field stance* can only be achieved by immersing yourself in the issues, attitudes, and language of the discipline.

While not exhaustive, the following literature review offers an excellent introduction to the critical conversation. When you read through Gislason's review, try to identify as many critical issues as you can. Ask yourself how and where you might enter the conversation. What issues sound like they have potential for future development? Which points sound like they have merit? Which do not? Have the critics missed an issue of potential importance? How might you frame and develop such an issue?

Box 2.1: Field Notes from Literary Criticism: How Readers Have Responded to Crane's "The Bride Comes to Yellow Sky"

Eric Gislason

R.M. Weatherford, in the introduction to his *Stephen Crane and the Critical Heritage*, writes that within months of Crane's death, he was "almost totally forgotten" (2). Many of Crane's contemporaries were more interested in how he lived than in what he wrote. During his lifetime, critics often concentrated on his daring journalistic exploits as a war correspondent in Cuba and Greece and his controversial lifestyle; they paid little attention to his writings, other than his novella, *The Red Badge of Courage*, published in 1895.

The Early Reviews

A few months after its initial appearance in *McClure's Magazine*, "The Bride" was included in *The Open Boat and Other Tales of Adventure* (1898). Reviews of this collection were generally favorable, but the collection failed to sell many copies. An unsigned review in the *Saturday Review* called "The Bride" "a singularly vivid and picturesque sketch of Texan life" (qtd. in Weatherford 222). Another unsigned review in the *Spectator* mentions the "humour of the strange home-coming of the town-marshal of Yellow Sky and his newly wedded wife" and concludes with the hope that more readers will become interested in Crane—"the most striking and irresistible of all the younger American writers" (223). Respected critics such as Harold Frederic and Edward Garnett hailed Crane as one of America's foremost writers, but their assessment was not widely shared (Weatherford 20). Garnett's review in the journal *Academy* contained high praise for "The Bride" in particular:

> In "The Bride Comes to Yellow Sky" ... the art is simply immense. There is a page and a half of conversation at the end of this short story of seventeen pages which, as a dialogue revealing the whole inside of the situation, is a lesson to any artist living. And the last line of this story, by the gift peculiar to the author of using some odd simile which cunningly condenses the feeling of the situation, defies analysis altogether. (228)

Garnett concluded his review by calling Crane "undoubtedly ... the genius" of the younger generation of American writers (229). Such praise for Crane's work was rare among his contemporaries, however.

The literary reputation of Stephen Crane would be made many years after his death.

To his contemporaries, Crane the man was much more interesting and noteworthy than Crane the artist. Richard Chase describes Crane as the man who "established the modern legend in this country of the literary bohemian—by consorting with low life, by asserting his isolation and intransigence in opposition to the conventionality of middle-class life" (v). When Crane died of tuberculosis at the young age of 29, his colourful reputation went with him, and his works were almost entirely unnoticed until the early 1920s. World War I inspired a reprinting of *The Red Badge of Courage*, but most of the stories that are acknowledged as masterpieces today—"The Open Boat," "The Blue Hotel," and "The Bride"—went largely unread.

Some Twentieth-Century Views

Crane's critical reputation began to change with the publication, in 1921, of an anthology of his stories called *Men, Women and Boats*. It did not include "The Bride," but it did attract new readers to Crane's work and showed them that he had written a good deal more than *The Red Badge of Courage*. In 1923, Thomas Beer published the first biography of Crane, an impressionistic portrait of the artist as a young, hard-living, bohemian genius (27). Beer's account sometimes played fast and loose with the facts of Crane's life, and its assertions often misled and confused subsequent efforts by Crane scholars. However, Beer's book was popular, and almost certainly served as one of the reasons for the 1926 publication of a twelve-volume edition of Crane's work featuring prefaces by well-known authors such as Willa Cather, H.L. Mencken, and Sherwood Anderson (Weatherford 28). Crane had been dead for a quarter-century, but his writings were receiving new attention.

Critical appreciation can be fickle, however. Although *The Red Badge of Courage* was reprinted during World War II and also appeared in Hemingway's 1942 anthology *Men at War*, it was not until the 1950s that Crane's fiction would finally begin to garner significant, widespread critical acclaim. John Berryman's 1950 biography of Crane approached his life and work from a Freudian perspective, and inspired new critical debates about its significance. A new generation of scholars began to re-examine Crane, and over the next twenty years there were hundreds of articles published on all aspects of his work. By the beginning of the 1970s, Crane, once almost completely forgotten, was now securely established as a major writer. As if to finalize this fact, and also to resolve considerable critical debate about the original texts of Crane's writings, the University Press of Virginia compiled and printed a ten-volume "definitive" edition of his works.

Sample Critical Issue

Critic Thomas A. Gullason summarizes the two main interpretations critics have made when approaching "The Bride." "For years," he writes, "'The Bride Comes to Yellow Sky' was read as a satiric comedy, or as a hilarious parody; lately, a few critics have challenged these readings by pointing to Crane's fundamental seriousness in the western tale" (407–9). Edwin Cady, for example, calls the story "a hilariously funny parody of neo-romantic lamentations over 'The Passing of the West'" (103). John Berryman suggests that "The Bride Comes to Yellow Sky" is a "singular vision of happiness," while A.M. Tibbetts refers to "The Bride" as "nearly pure comedy" (qtd. in Gullason 431). Other critics, such as Kenneth Bernard, find serious and tragic elements in the story. Bernard interprets the story as an "elegy" that "laments the passing of the old West and its values and deplores the rise of the new, 'civilized' values of the East" (435). Eric Solomon suggests that Crane's purpose in "The Bride" is to "cast a cold eye" on the myths of the Western hero and outlaw, and to show that the "weapons" of civilization are ultimately too much for Scratchy Wilson's revolvers (229).

By 1972, Tibbetts found himself defending a reading once taken for granted, arguing that most critics misread "The Bride" because they "try to interpret it as serious allegory instead of appreciating it as comedy" (qtd. in Gullason 430). Although Tibbetts agrees that "The Bride" is similar to other distinctly tragic Crane stories—"The Open Boat" and "The Blue Hotel," for example—he concludes that "The Bride" must be "read differently, for it is nearly pure comedy" (431). Crane's use of dramatic and ironic techniques in "Yellow Sky," Tibbetts argues, is "generally either overridden by comic effects or shaped for the ends of comedy" (432). The marshal and his bride are portrayed as ludicrous, out-of-place yokels in the plushy upholstered Pullman car, unaware that they are being mocked by their fellow passengers and by the Negro porter. Scratchy Wilson, in his bright shirt and red-topped boots, is a cartoon outlaw, a comical, non-threatening (though noisy) figure. The confrontation between the "ancient antagonists"—marshal and outlaw—is a humorous farce, a "burlesque of the Western feud" that ends comically when Scratchy is unable to comprehend the "foreign condition" of the Potters' marriage. For Tibbetts, the conclusion of the story "implies a happy ending," a new social order in which Scratchy Wilson will "reform and get religion," and the marshal and his new bride will live "happily ever after" (434). Tibbetts finds no evidence to suggest that the story ends on a tragic note.

Critics like Bernard and Solomon find Tibbetts's and Cady's readings of "The Bride" too sunny and optimistic. They argue that the story seems to be much more humorous than it actually is. Bernard argues that Crane's description of Marshal Potter's feelings aboard the train are overdone, too extreme for the purposes of comedy. Crane uses such overstatement to illuminate a fundamental change in Potter's social position—from marshal to husband.

It is probably fair to say that Crane himself was at least ambiguous about such change, and about the civilizing influences of the East. Consider the inscription Crane wrote in a book he gave to a fellow American writer: "To Hamlin Garland of the honest West, from Stephen Crane of the false East" (Berryman 97). Crane's sympathy with this "honest" West can be seen in his portrait of the demise of Scratchy Wilson and the muddled self-awareness of the married marshal—a newly minted representative of the "false" East.

Crane's complex story resists easy explanation and invites re-reading. This tour of critical responses to "The Bride" suggests some of the major issues confronting readers of the story, and familiarity with these responses should help you enrich and amplify your own experiences with Crane's "daisy."

Works Cited

Beer, Thomas. *Stephen Crane: A Study in American Letters*. 1923. New York: Octagon, 1980. Print.

Bernard, Kenneth. "'The Bride Comes to Yellow Sky': History as Elegy." *Stephen Crane's Career: Perspectives and Evaluations*. Ed. Thomas A. Gullason. New York: New York UP, 1972. 435–39. Print.

Berryman, John. *Stephen Crane*. 1950. Cleveland: World Publishing, 1962. Print.

Cady, Edwin. *Stephen Crane*. Boston: Twayne Publishers, 1980. Print.

Chase, Richard, ed. "Introduction." *The Red Badge of Courage and Other Writings*. Boston: Houghton, Mifflin, 1960. Print.

Gullason, Thomas A., ed. *Stephen Crane's Career: Perspectives and Evaluations*. New York: New York UP, 1972. Print.

Solomon, Eric. *Stephen Crane: From Parody to Realism*. Cambridge, MA: Harvard UP, 1966. Print.

Tibbetts, A.M. "'The Bride Comes to Yellow Sky' as Comedy," *Stephen Crane's Career: Perspectives and Evaluations*. Ed. Thomas A. Gullason. New York: New York UP, 1972. 430–34. Print.

Weatherford, Richard M., ed. *Stephen Crane: The Critical Heritage*. Boston: Routledge and Kegan Paul, 1973. Print.

"Fielding" Some Questions

Here are some initial points of entry into the critical conversation. If you've already begun to "mark up the text," including Gislason's literature review, you've probably generated an initial list of points and questions. The more you see, the sooner you'll find your own critical (or "field") stance. You can always *add to, redefine, argue against,* or *recontextualize* existing readings.

An important point to remember: *do not be intimidated by other readers' views.* Do not fall into the trap of feeling that others have already said all that can be said about the story. As we'll discuss in detail in the next chapter, there's always a "knowledge deficit"—a place with critical elbow room where you can develop your own interpretation. You may not be the first one to notice the curious image that ends "Yellow Sky," but, if it interests you, have faith that you can (with work) come up with an interpretation that contributes to the critical discussion. First, though, you need to *find your own issue.*

Consider the following observations and questions drawn from a reading of Eric Gislason's literature review. As you read these, see how many issues match your interests as a student critic.

1. Crane's work seems to have meant different things to different readers at different times. How would you characterize the trajectory of the critical conversation?

2. From the outset, readers have been interested in the story's humour. Did the story strike you as funny? Do some research

on *comedy* as a literary genre: what are the comic aspects of the story?

3. Many critics, including Gislason, seem intent on confirming Crane's literary reputation. What role does *evaluation* play in literary response?

4. Edward Garnett isolates an intriguing critical issue by suggesting that the last line of the story "defies analysis altogether." Do you agree?

5. Many critics seem particularly interested in or influenced by biographical details related to the author's brief life. Must we assume that Stephen Crane and the narrator are one and the same?

6. The University Press of Virginia "legitimized" Crane's work by compiling and printing an authoritative edition. (You may wish to compare his story in that edition with the original *McClure's Magazine* version printed in this book.) Why would one edition be considered more authoritative than another? What effect might editorial decisions/changes have on your reading of the story?

7. Critics in the 1970s begin to take issue with and redefine the story as "a comedy." What is at stake in redefining the genre? Can a story be both comedy and elegy?

8. A.M. Tibbetts echoes Garnett's interest in the story's ending, finding no evidence that "The Bride" ends on a tragic note. Where would a reader look for such evidence?

9. What patterns have the critics missed? Why does the newly married Potter feel like "a thief in the night" and a "traitor to Yellow Sky"? What do all the references to music signify? Why, in the story's final scene, is the bride described as "yellow as old cloth"? Why are there so many references to death? Why does the narrator pay so much attention to clothes? To water and liquid? What is the narrator's attitude throughout the story? Does it change?

10. What of the reader's response? Are there points in the story where we are more engaged? More detached? Why does the story affect us in this way?

Exercises

Social Stance and Institutional Stance

1. Discuss your list of issues with others in the class. Is there any consensus over which issues are important?

2. Reflect on the process you've used to identify important issues. Next, interview two people working in another discipline, say, geography or psychology, and ask them how they would approach these same issues. Report orally in class.

Textual Stance

1. In your response journal, take any textual pattern identified in Eric Gislason's essay and find as much evidence as you can that seems related to that pattern. Look for key quotations.

2. Take the evidence gathered and fashion it into a critical issue (you may want to jump ahead to Chapter 3 for further clarification of what constitutes a "critical issue").

Field Stance

1. The literature review tells a story of critical response, but it is not the only story. Go to the library and look up three or four of the essays that Gislason cites. See if he has highlighted the same points as you would have if you were writing your own literature review. Write a two-page reflection on what may have been left out or underemphasized.

2. Consult some of the critics that the review does not reference. Write a brief essay where you note any critical issues or insights left out.

CHAPTER 3

Writing the Critical Essay:
Form and the Critical Process

Overview

In this chapter, we explore the critical essay in terms of form and process. Once you've gathered your personal response notes, you'll need to shape them into an essay. The first half of this chapter, written especially for first-year university students, will help you understand the logic and conventions of that essay form; the second half, written with intermediate and senior-level students in mind, will help you understand more about the assumptions, methods, and approaches used by experienced critics.

Form

You've probably heard a variation of the old line, "I don't know much about art, but I know what I like when I see it." Many of us might not be able to define precisely all the elements that constitute a critical essay, but most of us know one when we see it. The *layout* alone is an important signal. These three different formats represent writing in English, the social sciences, and business:

As these thumbnail images illustrate, the layout of the English essay helps focus attention on the text. The layout, which keeps the literary text in the foreground as a clear reference, has its origins in biblical exegesis (the tradition of biblical interpretation). Ancient interpreters frequently placed the "sacred text" at the centre of the page, in a manner similar to today's block quotation. A church homily or sermon functions in the same way: the text is read out loud and then the religious leader offers the commentary.

The parallel between religious ritual and critical practice is no coincidence. The techniques and conventions of literary inquiry evolved from traditions of biblical interpretation. The first professors of English were usually clergymen with training in the classics. In the nineteenth century, some critics saw literature (and literary criticism) as a secular substitute for Christianity itself. Scrupulous attention to "the word," to getting the words right, remains a key aspect of critical writing.

The critical essay in English is full of quotations. Unlike the social sciences, where students are encouraged to paraphrase primary and secondary sources, English encourages much more direct quotation and discussion of those quotations. This formula of *quote-and-discuss* is traditional in English studies. It also replicates the process of reading, dramatizing the writer's response as "a reader of the text." In offering a critical discussion you are necessarily advocating a way of "reading the text," an argument about how the story can be read and understood. Be careful, though, not to provide a simple narration of your private reading process. A line-by-line or scene-by-scene discussion does not usually constitute a *critical* reading. It may make for a useful first draft, but it is not yet a critical essay. Instead, use your reading of key passages as evidence to support a guiding thesis, a literary argument that provides a framework for analyzing and interpreting the literary work.

Also, be careful not to provide a simple plot summary. Listen to Shakespeare professor Richard Marius on where many first essays go astray. Year after year he has received freshman papers that "do little more than summarize the plot or give us three reasons for believing that ambition is a theme in *Macbeth*" (376). Such papers, he says, lack an *organizing principle*:

> "Look, here in the beginning we find ambition in Macbeth when he meets the three witches. Look, here is ambition again when he writes to Lady Macbeth. Look, here it is again when they talk." We are walked through the paper as though we might be walked through an art gallery, our guide pointing out the various sights in a commentary shaped by the physical arrangement of the painting. (177)

Box 3.1: Field Notes from the Visual Arts: Visual Mapping

Many students find visual mapping (where you lay out the main elements of the story graphically on the page) a useful way of arranging evidence. The two examples pictured here are by students Charlotte Tetreau and Debbie Endean. The first traces the story's plot structure, paying particular attention to the triangular configurations of plot, imagery, and character relations; the second explores references to "time."

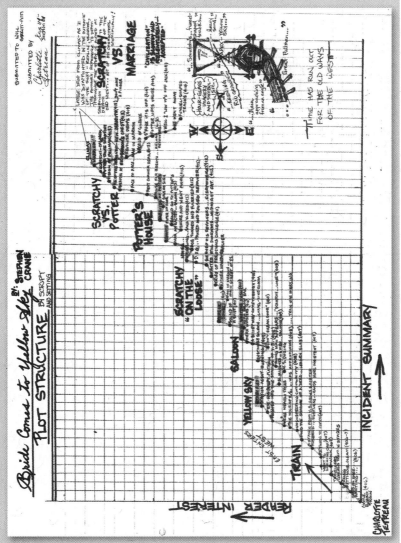

TIME and MOVEMENT IN

PART ONE ~ the journey begins.

"It's a thousand miles from one end of Texas to the other, and this train runs right across it and never stops but four times."

PART TWO
3:21 – "The California Express was due at Yellow Sky in twenty-one minutes."

THE BRIDE COMES TO YELLOW SKY
by Stephen Crane

PART THREE

"Yellow Sky was dozing."

"... sag glowed drowsily"

PART FOUR
3:42

The End of the journey...

WEST vs. EAST

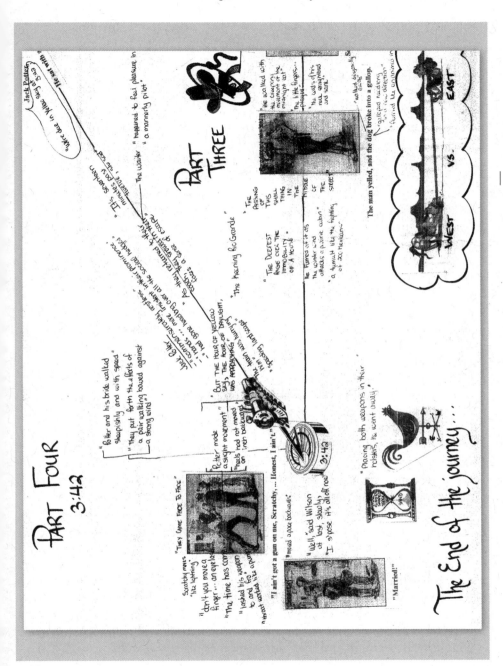

Marius's notion of the critic as gallery guide is a useful one. Imagine the difference between the kind of tour offered by a novice guide and, say, one offered by an art historian. The novice might be tempted to comment briefly on each exhibit in the order it has been displayed. The novice *surveys* the evidence. In contrast, the expert may make passing comment on the exhibition as a whole, but she is likely to concentrate on those exhibits that fit the story she wishes to tell. The expert says more about less; the expert selects and *arranges* the evidence to suit his or her viewpoint. In other words, you need not tie your discussion to the chronology of the story.

Feel free to start your essay with a key scene, moment, or word from the middle or the end—or any part of the story that especially interests you. Arrange your discussion of the text according to the logic of your essay, not according to the order of the plot. A "tour" of Crane's "The Bride Comes to Yellow Sky," for example, might focus on any number of issues. Textual issues would include your interpretation of key image patterns, of key scenes, of character development, of how setting works, etc. Sometimes instructors assign topics that force such a focus: "Write an essay discussing characterization in ..." or "Write an essay on setting in ...." Such topics invite a focus on literary form and may seem to encourage the piling up of undifferentiated examples that disappoints professors such as Richard Marius; these topics can become the basis for an essay only when they are linked to critical issues.

In its simplest form, the critical issue is a problem (usually presented in your introduction) that your essay resolves through careful interpretation of the literary text. The more focused your problem, the better your chance of writing a successful essay. The Kolb interview describes a three-stage process for defining the critical issue: (1) organize your general response notes into an "area" of investigation (such as point of view, imagery, style, or historical context); (2) find a specific "topic" within that area (such as how point of view, imagery, etc., contribute to our interpretation of the story); and (3) decide on a "thesis" (that is, what you intend to argue by exploring your topic). Remember to trust your intuition when first coming to terms with the critical issue. Ask yourself which topics or patterns challenge your expectations: a topic that you find initially unsettling will help focus your critical attention and likely interest other readers as well.

An even more advanced form of the critical issue requires a secure field stance, where you work out your own interpretation and then insert it into the ongoing critical conversation. Note that this approach need not entail as thorough a review as that of Eric Gislason in Chapter 2. In fact, some instructors may at first encourage their students not to use the work of other critics—or to use no more than two or three. They want to hear *your* interpretations before encouraging any comparing of notes with other critics. Nonetheless, it is important that you be aware of the full critical writing process, and background research is essential to that process.

In classes beyond the introductory level, instructors will expect you to explore the critical literature. Research and an awareness of developments in the field are central to both the institutional and the field stances. Begin by discussing the topic with others (that is, enter the classroom conversation), and then, with guidance from your instructor, look up several published interpretations and note how they either confirm or contradict your reading of the story. Try to find some critical elbow room for your interpretation: assert an angle on the critical issue that has not been fully explored or developed by other critics.

Exercises

Social and Institutional Stances

1. Discuss the notion of "critical issues" with others in class. Do you find any consensus regarding what constitutes a critical issue in literary studies?

2. Interview one student and one faculty member from a discipline outside the humanities: share the definition of a critical issue offered in this chapter and ask both whether they agree with the definition. How would they go about establishing what's already been said or written about a critical issue in their field? Prepare an oral report on your results.

Textual and Field Stances

1. Go to the library and locate two critical journals. Read the opening sections (the first page or so) of two or three articles and analyze how the critics define their issues and acknowledge the work of other critics. In your response journal, write a two-paragraph discussion of the strategies observed.

2. Interview a member of the English faculty and ask how he or she decided on a dissertation topic in graduate school. Find out what issue the dissertation explored, why the issue was important, and what the faculty member said that was new or valuable about the issue. Write a brief report and share your results with the class.

3. Go to the University of Pennsylvania's Call for Papers Site: http://call-for-papers.sas.upenn.edu/. Click on a topic under the "Categories" heading and read a sampling of the requests for contributions to academic conferences and publications. What issues seem especially current? Which critical issues seem to provoke the most interest among literary scholars? In your response journal, write a two-paragraph analysis of the *areas*, *issues*, and *approaches* addressed in three or four Calls for Papers. Note: many of the calls have their own website addresses attached to the request. Try tracking down one or two of these sites so you can explore the rationale and context for the request. Add your impressions to your response journal and discuss any interesting critical issues with your instructor.

How to Move from an "F" to an "A": Modelling the Process

Here we will go step-by-step through the process of (1) identifying and exploring a critical issue, (2) finding the right approach to develop the issue, and (3) making sure that resolving the issue makes some contribution to the field. First we need to see how we might take a failing opening paragraph and turn it into a first-class piece of work. Using examples from actual student essays, I'll demonstrate and discuss the process of successful *revision*. We'll also consider the "six common places of literary criticism," the central areas of concern and inquiry among professional critics. Understanding how these common places function will help you gain even greater insight into the critical process. The chapter concludes with some words about differing critical approaches and methods you can use to write more fully developed essays.

Writing and Rewriting

To paraphrase cultural anthropologist Clifford Geertz, if you want to understand what literary criticism is, "you should look in the first instance not at its theories or findings; ... you should look at what the practitioners of it do" (5). One of the central things that literary critics do is write essays on literature. Critics employ a variety of techniques in an effort to interpret and share what are seen as either personally significant or culturally significant texts. Geertz reminds us, though, that what we do is not simply a matter of methods—though practising different methods is important. What defines literary criticism "is the kind of intellectual effort it is" (6). That is, we need to see the methods in action and understand them as part of a complex mode of intellectual inquiry. We need to understand what motivates the methods.

Many very intelligent and talented student writers become frustrated when they find themselves unable to take the "next step" in their writing. While it may seem relatively obvious how to move from an F paper to a C paper, the route from a B to an A is not always so clear. Being able to write well is important, but you also need to learn to *think critically*. You need to enter the field.

Those whose critical writing remains removed from field concerns seldom find strong critical issues to address. The social, institutional, and textual stances will enable you to identify, organize, and discuss key patterns—but the "critical issue" may elude you. You may find yourself simply going through the motions without ever developing a clear critical position. To develop a field stance you'll need to look even more closely at what critics do and how they do it. Let's begin with examples of critical writing from four student writers.

Most instructors of English have internalized the features of a successful critical essay. Many believe they can tell an A paper from a C paper after reading only the opening paragraph. Defining your purpose clearly from the outset will make the best impression, and this takes time and intellectual effort. This is why many critics write their *opening* statements near the *end* of the writing process.

The following sample introductions are arranged in ascending order of quality, ranging from unsuccessful to excellent. Each version is an amalgam of actual writing handed in by first- and second-year English students. As you read these, see how the theme of "change" develops from essay to essay. See how the more successful versions specify that theme and link it to (1) a particular pattern, and (2), in at least one case, a clear critical issue.

VERSION #1

After my first reading of Stephen Crane's short story "The Bride Comes to Yellow Sky," I found it difficult to take in, all at once, what

Crane was trying to express. After reading the story a few more times, and asking myself some questions as to why Crane wrote what he did, the meaning of the story became clearer. Crane writes with very few words yet he expresses so much. The short story, "The Bride Comes to Yellow Sky," can be interpreted in many ways by different readers. This short story has many themes. I managed to find one theme which I thought Crane was trying to express the most among all the others. This main theme is that the old Western ways cannot last forever. This main theme is shown in Crane's work through his characters and his imagery.

VERSION #2

One theme in Stephen Crane's "The Bride Comes to Yellow Sky" is change. Sheriff Potter shows a fear of change when he is confronted by the effects of his marriage. In the story Crane uses references to change to emphasize this sense of anxiety. Crane sets out the change theme right away in the story when he describes the "plains of Texas … pouring eastward." The life Potter has known is "sweeping into the east, sweeping over the horizon, a precipice." On board the train Potter looks nervous "like a man waiting in a barber's shop." We normally think of children rather than adults being nervous about getting a haircut, so we know a major change is taking place.

VERSION #3

Throughout Stephen Crane's "The Bride Comes to Yellow Sky" there appear numerous images of change which serve to isolate the story's protagonist, Sheriff Potter, and magnify his sense of guilt in contributing to that change. The West, represented by Potter's hometown of Yellow Sky, is in a period of transition—and Potter's recent marriage is an important factor in that transition. Despite the "elation" he feels about "the glory of their marriage," as he draws closer to home, Potter begins to feel a mixture of embarrassment, shame, and fear. Like one who has "committed an extraordinary crime," he feels like someone "bringing his bride before an innocent and unsuspecting community." Part One of the story thus sets up an internal conflict where the central character seems caught in a moment of personal and communal transition. The "new estate" of marriage brings with it Eastern ways and values, ways and values that by the end of the story come into open conflict with those of the Old West.

VERSION #4

Stephen Crane's "The Bride Comes to Yellow Sky" offers a gently grieving elegy for the passing of the old West, but it is an elegy punctuated by a sometimes comic, sometimes condescending narrative tone. At one point in the story, while the protagonist, Sheriff Potter, and his bride are on board the train, a passenger is described as growing "excessively sardonic," winking "at himself in one of the numerous mirrors." This curiously incongruous image, suggesting both emotional involvement and ironic detachment, captures a certain narrative ambivalence. This is a story about two world views (the new East and the old West) in conflict, and I find it intriguing how that ambivalence informs virtually all of the key images. In Part One alone, the train that carries Potter and the bride to Yellow Sky is said to "whirl" with "dignity of motion"; the coach's fittings shine "as darkly brilliant as a pool of oil"; Potter's face shines, "elated" by his marriage, yet frowns as he finds "the shadow of a deed weigh upon him like a leaden slab." Just as it is difficult to "whirl" with "dignity"—or to shine "darkly brilliant"—Sheriff Potter finds himself a man in transition, moving uncomfortably between darkness and light, the old and the new.

Note: *Before reading the commentary section, draw your own conclusions about the relative merit of each version. Why would the critical community be likely to find version #4 more successful than version #1? Where would you rank your own critical writing?*

Commentary

All four versions have their strong points, but they are not equally successful as samples of critical writing.

Version #1 presents a narrative of reader response and is actually a typical "first essay." Shortly before this essay was written, we had talked in class about "reading" literature—and this student became sidetracked in telling the story of his own initial difficulty in reading "The Bride." I suspect that the references to multiple readings, and the acknowledgement that multiple interpretations and themes are possible, are meant to persuade me (i.e., the instructor) that the author had understood the lectures and class discussion. The author adopts a social stance (writing for a specific teacher), but seems to have started writing at the response stage without (or before) having

| 49 |

delved into the critical literature in the field and without having developed a personal viewpoint informed by that research. This essay misses the critical mark: it talks about the reading process, which is only the first step in the critical process, and discusses the text in such general terms that it ends up contributing very little. Try changing all the references to the story's title and author from "The Bride" and "Crane" to any other title and author. Very little in this introduction seems specific to "The Bride Comes to Yellow Sky." It could be about almost any story. The essay is made general, also, by an absence of direct quotation. Most instructors would rate this writing in the F to D range.

Version #2 does focus, in specific terms, on Crane's story. Like the first version, it discusses the theme of change, but it also links that theme to the Potters' marriage. Having introduced this link, however, the essay jumps to two indirectly related examples: the changing view from the train and Potter's uncharacteristic nervousness, as though the student is still exploring the topic and finding examples that may build to a point of view. Instead of "building" on an interpretation, the writer has started at the beginning of the story, looking for examples in the order in which they appear. Quotations are used as examples, but they are not presented clearly within the logic of an argument. There is better balance between the social and textual stances than in version #1, but the writing lacks a field orientation. Most instructors would rate writing like this in the C to C+ range.

In Version #3 the student has learned from research that there are various ways of viewing change in the story, has settled on one that can be argued for, and takes the connection between "change" and Potter's nervousness as its principal point of departure for an interpretation of the story. It specifies the nature of the change taking place ("The West is in a period of transition") and suggests that the "marriage is an important factor in that transition." Potter's anxiety is explained as a kind of subconscious acknowledgement of culpability: in bringing his bride home to Yellow Sky, he is helping usher in a new age of domesticity and civilization. The sample compares Potter's internal conflict with the external conflict, the "showdown" between East and West that concludes the story. Quotations are used as evidence to support this interpretation, the writing is straightforward, and we get a clear sense of where the argument is going. This introduction shows a much wider understanding of the social, textual, and field stances than either version #1 or version #2. Most instructors would rate writing like this in the B range.

Version #4 demonstrates that the student has explored the subject to the point where the observations encompass and *transcend* the critical sources. The student is in a position to state the theme of change clearly and confidently: the story presents "a gently grieving elegy for the passing of the Old West." In addition, the introduction not only focuses on a pattern, but also establishes a critical issue: it tells us something new (i.e., of interest to the field) about Crane's use of imagery and how that imagery creates a narrative ambivalent toward the changing face of the Old West. The writer is personally engaged ("I find it intriguing how ..."), moves from specific example (the passenger winking) to a general pattern (of paradoxical imagery), and integrates quotations as textual support for the interpretation offered. More useful still, this version shows how imagery, narrative point of view, characterization, and theme are interconnected: all share an element of ambiguity, as if neither the narrator nor the sheriff has made up his mind about the pros and cons of an encroaching Eastern civilization. The quotations are elegantly integrated and discussed: the author uses the quotations as textual support—*and* as primary evidence to be analyzed and discussed. Instructors should rate writing like this in the A to A+ range.

| 51 |

The next step is to take version #4 and develop the critical issue even further. To do so, we need to focus on *field* concerns:

- a detailed review of where critics turn to develop their interpretations
- a consideration of several key critical approaches
- a check of how our interpretation fits into the "conversation" of published critical responses

The Six Common Places of Literary Criticism

Ancient Greek rhetoric defined a grouping of strategies called *topoi* or "places" that any educated person might call upon to argue a case. The ancients seemed to believe in an actual place in the mind where ideas might be stored and retrieved. In more practical terms, the *topoi* were used as a way of coming up with ideas—as strategies or probes for exploring a subject or developing an argument. Aristotle developed a list of 28 such *topoi* as resources for developing arguments, but these *topoi* are probably familiar to you as the common ways we organize essays: by comparison/contrast, by definition, through demonstrating cause and effect, and by division.

Academic disciplines have developed their own "places in the mind," literally "common places" where scholars turn to *understand*, *analyze*, *interpret*, and *evaluate* complex works of literature.

Two contemporary rhetoricians, Jeanne Fahnestock and Marie Secor, have emphasized six of these *topoi*, which they consider to be fundamental and field specific:

- Contemptus Mundi
- Complexity
- Appearance/Reality
- Everywhereness
- Paradigm
- Paradox

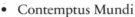

Learning more about the *topoi* will help you understand how critics focus and organize their interpretations. Using the *topoi* will help you select a topic and develop it fully.

The six *topoi* often overlap, but in most cases we should be able to see an emphasis on one or two in any successful interpretation. These *topoi*, remember, reflect shared (although sometimes unspoken) assumptions about the nature of the reader, the writer, the text, and the social context. These shared assumptions define the critical community and help shape the critical conversation.

Contemptus Mundi *and Complexity*

These two common places reflect the critical values (1) that the modern world is a place of decay, alienation, and anxiety; and (2) that the meaning of literature is complex and thus requires careful and sensitive interpretation. These topoi help us identify the story's theme.

Who hasn't heard the expression "things aren't like they used to be"? Most of us, at one time or another, have lamented about how modern styles or technologies have changed life for the worse. When you express such sentiments, you are using the *contemptus mundi topos*.

The notion that the best literature, and art generally, should be complex and thus requires sustained interpretation, is another idea central to the contemporary critical mindset. After all, says the critic, why waste time considering a work that is so simple that its meaning is self-evident? When you seek out works that challenge both intellect and imagination, you are using the complexity *topos*.

The general theme of "The Bride Comes to Yellow Sky" (the passing away of old traditions) and the story's layering of multiple meanings match our first two *topoi*. As I've already noted, the critical community's values affect how works are interpreted. A certain scep-ticism about the inherent value of progress seems common in literary studies—and thus many critics would see "The Bride" as a "loss of innocence" story. They would sympathize with those who are most affected by industrial change.

On the other hand, the range of viewpoints represented (those of the narrator, the sheriff, the bride, the train passengers, the porter, the townsfolk, and the drummer) suggests that not all in the story are in agreement over what has been lost and what has been won (or found). The theme may be familiar, but its presentation is ambivalent. Its complexity makes it attractive to literary critics.

Appearance/Reality

This common place assumes the presence of "hidden meaning," of both a surface-level meaning and a deeper meaning. Patterns of duality tend to support such a critical view.

Many students starting out in their first literature class tend to think that "digging for meaning" is what English is *all* about. Some become intimidated, feeling that they'll never see all those hidden patterns— and they end up suspecting that those who do find such patterns are really "reading in" too much. A frequent question is this: "Did the author really put all those patterns into the work?" Others, of course, delight in discovering layers of meaning in a story, novel, or poem. When you focus on two of these layers, a surface meaning and a deep meaning, you are using the appearance/reality *topos*.

Fahnestock and Secor locate the critical interest in duality as the "most prevalent special *topos*." While recognizing that duality takes many forms (inner/outer, depth/surface, subject/object), they argue for a general category of shared assumptions that characterizes this *topos*. "We might even claim," they say, "that the Appearance/Reality *topos* is the fundamental assumption of criticism, since without it there would be no impetus to analyze or interpret literature" (85).

The search for meanings, whether in terms of image patterns, literary allusions, or embedded ideologies, is an important feature of critical writing. In version #4, the West/East or old/new conflict is shown to be central to the story. Indeed, we can argue that the climax of the story hinges not only on a failed gunfight, but on a showdown between Western traditions and encroaching Eastern values: the failed gunfight (the appearance) highlights the West's failure to resist Eastern influence (the larger reality). Were we to develop the Appearance/Reality *topos* further, we'd want to catalogue how a general pattern of duality is reflected in or supported by such elements as plot structure, setting, atmosphere, characterization, imagery, and narrative point of view.

Everywhereness

This common place is central to any formalist critical approach. The idea is to find an important moment in, or feature of, the story that others may not have noticed—and then to find variations of it throughout the text.

Of the six *topoi*, the so-called everywhereness common place is perhaps the most fun because it is the most challenging. We are all familiar with buying a new shirt, or shoes, or car, only to start seeing the same style or model "everywhere." We do something similar for criticism if, when interpreting literature, we note a pattern that has gone unnoticed by others, and then show how the once-unnoticed aspect takes on a significant role as a carrier of meaning in the story.

The everywhereness *topos* seems already in play in the version #4 draft paragraph. By linking the mirror scene to a pattern of similarly ambiguous images, the paragraph fulfils a critical imperative: to discover a pattern of significance in some word, image, scene, action, or attitude that no one else has recognized—and to show how that pattern informs the entire story.

As Fahnestock and Secor tell us, "one of the most persuasive endeavours that a literary scholar can engage in is to find something (a device, an image, a linguistic feature, a pattern) that no one else has seen—and to find it everywhere" (87). The mirror scene actually brings together the everywhereness *topos* and the appearance/reality *topos*: to find a "startling duality" everywhere in the story is an acute observation.

To develop the everywhereness *topos* further, we'd need to note and discuss as many relevant examples as reasonably possible.

Our goal would be to show how the pattern of references supports the story's theme and affects our interpretation of that theme. For example, few readers would give much initial thought to all the time references in the first part of the story: the arrival time of the train, the silver watch, the hour of daylight approaching, etc. However, someone interested in this pattern of references might point out that they help set up the story's final image, where Scratchy Wilson's feet make "funnel-shaped tracks in the heavy sand." Like the references to the watch and the hour, the final scene's linking of the funnel-shape and sand presents us with another time image—that of an hourglass, suggesting that Scratchy's time has run out.

| 55 |

Paradigm

This common place relates the structure of the text to the structure of the world. The critical objective is to find important and revealing correspondences.

This common place is a little more difficult to understand, at least at first. We all know that our past experiences help shape our understanding of anything new. When those past experiences become the basis for a philosophy or world view, they tend to "frame" our understanding even further. Those using the paradigm *topos* compare and contrast patterns of lived experience with patterns found in the text.

The paradigm *topos* asks us to look for a real-world template (a mental, historical, aesthetic, or political reality) that might help order or explain the story. When we employ the paradigm *topos* we seek parallels between the world and the literary work, or between a small structural unit in the work and some larger truth about the nature of art or the nature of interpretation. It is often said, for example, that the text teaches us how it should be read—that it provides cues for reader response. A key scene or image may work as such a guide to reading.

The man winking at himself in the mirror might echo the reader's complex relationship to the characters and their story. Like the man on the train, the reader sympathizes with the newly married pair. But we also remain detached, amused, and comparatively knowledgeable about both marriage and history in ways that the couple does not share.

Our position as fellow passengers (and commentators) is even more complex, though. The man's wink is described as "excessively sardonic," that is, "heartless." This characterization (a rebuke to the man in the mirror) keeps us in on the joke (we are amused by the out-of-place newlyweds) but distanced from the winking man's derisive gesture. We are asked to assume duality in our reading stance.

To develop the paradigm *topos* further, we'd need to explore how the mirror scene (or any similar key moment) relates in detail to either the reader's position or the author's position. We might speculate, for example, about the complex nature of either our reading experience or Crane's world view as an author.

Conversely, we can read the world back into the text: we could find a set of assumptions (a theory or ideology, for instance) and show how it is echoed in the mirror scene. A Marxist reader, for example, might see the politics of class struggle in the man's bourgeois, condescending wink. Another reader might note the mirror scene as evidence of the kind of self-consciousness we normally associate with late twentieth-century fiction. Someone else might consider how the optics of reflection play themselves out in other aspects of the story— how, for example, the reversed image we see in a mirror might relate to the numerous reversals of plot, character, social status, and reader expectations we find in the story.

Paradox

This common place focuses on those aspects of the story that seem illogical or contradictory, but turn out to be logical or true. Typically, critics use the paradox topos *to show how contradictory elements can be unified via creative interpretation.*

In everyday life, most of us don't go out looking for paradoxes. We prefer straightforward, unambiguous communication. For the literary critic, however, a paradox provides evidence of "complexity"—a more profound expression of reality—and thus of literary value.

An exploration of the paradox *topos* is central to version #4. Critics are especially fond of paradoxes—of finding ways to unify two apparently opposing views or images. One critic and teacher, Harvey Birenbaum, tells his students that the best way to begin an essay is by focusing on a paradox. He calls this strategy "the perfect beginning.... *The best thesis is a paradox*," he writes. "Why? Because, first of all, good literature commonly expresses a paradoxical view of life, and secondly, because the techniques of literature are in themselves interestingly paradoxical" (206).

If we look too closely at Birenbaum's advice, the logic begins to sound rather circular: literature holds a paradoxical view because it employs paradoxical techniques. As a strategy for writing essays, however, Birenbaum's reasoning seems unassailable: "A good thesis statement cannot be self-evident; it is controversial and risky, crying out for a defense. That is why paradoxical theses can be especially strong: they sound tantalizingly illogical and need to be justified" (206). For example, we might argue that "In 'The Bride Comes to Yellow Sky,' the death of Western traditions opens the way for a new social order of manners, women, and civilization; yet that death is a final defeat for freedom and naturalism."

Birenbaum goes on to link the Appearance/Reality *topos* to his call for a paradoxical thesis, offering us the following formula: "Although such and such seems to be the case, it eventually becomes clear that the truth is exactly the opposite" (207). Thus, were we to develop the paradox *topos* further, we might argue that "The old gun-fighter, Scratchy Wilson, seems the most vital, the most authentically Western of all the characters. Yet, by the end of the story, we discover that Wilson has become hopelessly out of place in the changing cultural landscape of Yellow Sky."

Critics seek meaning by identifying textual patterns—or by showing how those textual patterns reflect or illuminate our everyday world. The more complex the work, the more it is likely to be admired by literary critics. The six *topoi*, or critical common places, suggest fundamental shared assumptions among literary critics. Learning to recognize and explore these common places will help you develop your own field stance.

Critical Approaches

Once you have worked out a critical issue and used the six critical common places to guide the gathering of evidence, you may wish to take a step back and consider your *critical approach*. Professional critics align their work with certain schools of thought. They make public their assumptions regarding (1) the nature of the text, (2) the value of the text, and (3) how we read the text. These assumptions or theories guide both the critical approach taken and the methods employed.

One need not adhere religiously to any one approach; indeed, as the interview with Harold Kolb, Jr. testifies, critics tend to mix and match approaches depending on their objectives and the complexity of the issues under consideration. But even as student critics, you need to engage in some degree of reflection: there's no point owning a critical tool box if you don't look inside and discover how the tools work. You'll never learn which tools work best unless you try them out. Choosing a critical approach should help you clarify and organize your interpretations. As a student critic, your attention to critical approaches can suggest a range of available *methodologies*, new ways to gather insights and shape your readings.

In very general terms, we can divide the major critical approaches into three areas: those that find meaning residing *in the text*, those that find meaning residing in *the interaction of reader and text*, and those that find meaning *residing in the cultural context*. The first area is described as *formalist* and advocates close reading, which is interested primarily in literary form and content. The second area is described as *reader-response criticism*, which is interested in the ways in which readers variously bring meaning to texts and respond to textual features. The third area is described as *cultural criticism*, which is interested in how social, historical, political, and cultural forces shape both the production and reception of literature.

The brief survey that follows cannot tell you everything about literary theories and approaches, but perhaps it will whet your appetite to learn more and provide you with a practical introduction to a rich and varied component of literary criticism. We'll begin with the formalist approaches, not because they are the most important but because all of the other approaches are either a reaction against or an extension of close-reading techniques.

Mining the Text

Formalism: New Criticism and Deconstruction

New Critical inquiry and deconstruction are usually regarded as philosophical opposites: one seeks to find textual coherence by finding *unity of effect* among the formal elements; the other seeks to unravel any pretense of textual unity. In practice, however, both approaches stress close-reading techniques.

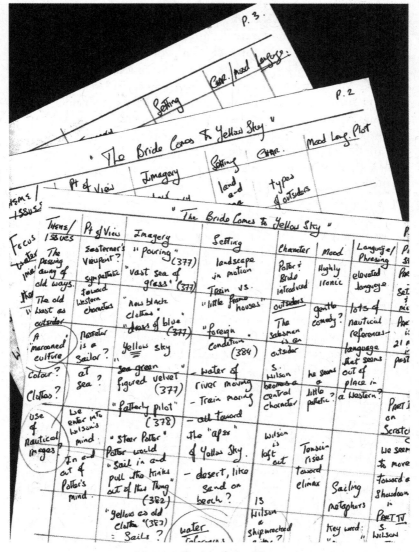

Literary Concordance Notes

New Criticism employs all six of the critical common places, but it tends to emphasize three: everywhereness, appearance/reality, and paradox. The New Critical method assumes that any personal response to literature is prompted by the work's formal elements. The principal task here is an analysis of these elements, showing how they work together to produce meaning. Kenneth Burke, who was not a New Critic himself, formulated what he called "the principle of literary concordance" (*Terms* 145), a concise statement of how formalist critics work.

According to Burke, the logical extension of the analytical model demands that we create an elaborate concordance (a system of cross-referencing) for every key word, image, or pattern. As intimidating as such a procedure sounds, in practice it is remarkably effective. Many of my own students have had considerable success by creating such concordances and grouping the results under formal headings: setting, point of view, imagery, characterization, and so on. The procedure may take up three or four pages of notes, but when you are finished you'll find that the concordance has helped organize your textual evidence. Lydia Marston's essay in Chapter 4, with its highly original reading of the word "maroon," is an example of this approach in action.

Such close-reading techniques seem "natural" to many readers. We've already discussed how reading involves a process of prediction, where the reader proceeds through the text by asking questions and guessing what comes next, sampling just enough of the text to confirm his or her predictions. We *bring* meaning to the text. Psycholinguist Frank Smith defines prediction as "the prior elimination of unlikely alternatives" (62), and if we expect to find unity, then we will be "unlikely" to find many contrary elements. Forcing coherence on texts—finding unity among the text's formal elements—reflects our tendency to find what we expect to see.

Deconstruction promotes an "unnatural" reading process, one designed to interrogate the text's premises and make the reader uncomfortable with *prior assumptions, hierarchies,* and *binary oppositions.* In other words, deconstruction asks us to question the basis of our predictions. Deconstruction gives attention to those "unlikely alternatives" made invisible by more conventional reading strategies. The goal here is to find the meaning beneath the meaning—or to show that the text doesn't really mean what many think it means.

Although it sounds a bit complicated, the *deconstructive method* is relatively straightforward and worth trying out. Thomas Fink has put together a wonderfully practical "How to Deconstruct" recipe. He divides the process into three critical moves:

1 Preliminary Phase

1.1 We use the appearance/reality *topos*, finding in the text patterns of dualities: good/evil, body/soul, light/dark, male/female, truth/fiction, old/new, etc. (Note that many of these pairs would work well for Crane's story.)

1.2 Next, we arrange these "binary" oppositions, determining the "superiority of one term over the other" as they work within the story.

2 Phase One

2.1 Find as many examples as you can where "the 'lower' term 'trades places' with the higher one."

2.2 Ask yourself what happens in the text that allows this trading of places. Look at each example individually.

3 Phase Two

3.1 Look for a pattern of words, actions, or images related to each term.

3.2 Choose a particular theme, idea, problem, or question in the text that has something to do with the binary opposition. Discuss this theme, idea, etc., by describing how words in the chain (that you chose in 3.1) relate to and contrast with one another. (Adapted from Fink 70).

For example, our version #4 text identifies two worlds in conflict, the East and the West. The West, it would seem, is being variously swept away or drowned by Eastern influences in the passage of time. The East, symbolized by the train, is linked to images of motion, power, and light; the West, to images of stasis, frailty, and darkness. At first glance, then, the East dominates the West.

As we apply the deconstructive approach, however, we look for places where the West asserts itself as the superior term—and there are a stunning number of reversals in the story.

The sheriff, someone of significance in his small corner of the world, seems hopelessly out of place (even comical) on board the train; yet the moment the train arrives in Yellow Sky, the porter treats him with some measure of deference: Potter regains some of his social status. The drummer (an Eastern salesman) seems in charge of the scene at the beginning of Part II—until the threat of Scratchy Wilson appears and casts the drummer into the role of "foreigner," someone as out of place in the "Weary Gentleman" Saloon as Potter is on the train. And Scratchy Wilson seems right at home until he comes face to face with Potter's marriage—and is made to feel like an outsider as well. This is a story of shifting social status, of changing places.

Next, we take each of these reversals and examine them in context, asking what allows the change in roles or status. Finally, we can examine each reversal as it relates to a significant binary pattern, such as the images of light and dark. A deconstructive reading might show the dark side of Potter's shining face, or of Yellow Sky's "new dawn." All that glitters in Yellow Sky is not golden; the reality, as the bride discovers, can make one's face turn "as yellow as old cloth."

We might want to show how the initially negative images of darkness ("a thief in the night") become positive; or why many readers would not celebrate the shining Eastern presence among the dozing residents of the old Western town. We might also want to note that neither East nor West, light nor dark, "wins" out over the other. Like oil and water (two important images in the story), East and West cannot be unified.

Deconstruction helps us avoid settling for easy answers. In short, the deconstructive approach gives us a method for explicating more fully what some readers might see as resolved dualities.

Reading Yourself into the Text

Reader-Response Criticism

The *reader-response approach* makes use of both the paradigm *topos* and the everywhereness *topos.* It looks at meaning as something created by the reader. The critical movement is *from* reader *to* text. Reader-response critics do not ignore form; they simply redefine it as something best understood in terms of its effect on reading: form is "an arousing and fulfillment of desires. A work has form insofar as one part of it leads a reader to anticipate another part, to be gratified by the sequence" (Burke, *Counter-Statement* 124).

In practice, reader-response approaches begin with a personal reaction to the text: how the story (or the elements that constitute the story) affects the reader is of primary importance. Next, you explore *how* its elements create *horizons of expectations* that the text either fulfils or denies. For instance, most readers familiar with the conventions of Westerns and gunfights would *expect* the story to climax in a showdown between Potter and Wilson (the new East and the old West)—but this gunfight never occurs. The reader-response approach would detail how the text and the reader conspire to create such expectations, and then explain what effect the denial of such expectations has on our understanding of the story.

Thus, for example, the *anti-climax* helps us recognize that, if we thought we were reading a conventional Western, we were being distracted from another more subtle, more interesting story. Potter's bravery expresses itself not in gunplay, but at the moment he publicly acknowledges his marriage. "Yes, I'm married," he tells Wilson three times in a row. This is the first time in the story that he stops hiding, stops feeling embarrassed. It is as if the full significance of the marriage "dawns" on him and the reader at the same moment. Like Potter, the reader's horizons of expectation remain tied to an understanding of Western motifs and clichés. The ending thus takes us by surprise.

In practice, the reader-response critic tends to look backward, first noting an interesting or unsettling personal reaction and then turning to the text to find what elements might have stimulated such a reaction. The reader's level of interest in the story—how engaged or detached you feel as your reading progresses—becomes a kind of critical barometer. The reading experience becomes highly self-conscious: you need to be able to step back and watch yourself reading, considering why the text has a certain effect on you, and how your prior experiences and frame of mind allow you to react in the way you do.

In summary, this self-conscious response strategy asks you to (1) record your reactions, (2) document your reading process, (3) identify elements of the text (plot structure, description, patterning) that might provoke your reactions, and (4) share your findings via a "response statement" (a protocol of your interaction with the text) or an interpretation based on your analysis of your reading process. Reader-response criticism tries to keep the experience of reading front and centre. If we push this approach further, if we consider what forces (ideological, historical, etc.) might shape our personal reactions, we move into the domain of cultural criticism.

Cultural Criticism

Finding the Right Critical Lens

New Historicism, Feminist Criticism, Myth Criticism, and Marxist Criticism are four of the more prominent varieties of the *cultural approach*. They emphasize the paradigm *topos*, viewing the text through a lens of a particular *world view* (a theory of the way the world works).

In some ways, this approach is the easiest to describe here because this book is based on such an approach. We have been examining the act of writing critical essays in terms of the social, institutional, textual, and field contexts. Although the terms may differ, variations of these same four contexts are used by cultural critics. This group of critics tends to emphasize the historical, institutional, textual, and ideological lenses we use to construct and interpret literature.

For example, a New Historicist believes that all stories are *constructed* out of a set of historical circumstances. To understand a work like "The Bride," which depicts a particular historical period, the New Historicist tries to recreate the historical, institutional, textual, and ideological circumstances of both its composition and the period depicted (see the interview with Kolb for a description of this process).

Cultural critics would be interested in the role women played in the historical development of the West; they would be interested in "unpacking" the narrator's comment that "Historically there was supposed to be something infinitely humorous in ... [the newly married couple's] situation." Likewise, if we take the mirror scene described in version #4, we might reconsider it through a New Historicist lens, looking at the historical period, the economic and technological inequities, the language, and the characters' assumptions—all as elements of *power politics*.

Critic George Monteiro writes that, in "The Bride," *social codes* and *contexts* situate each conflict and determine whether each character is to be "victim or victor":

> In the parlor-car world Potter is victim because choosing to live by the manners and mores of that world, he is at the moment less qualified to do so than the porter or the other passengers, for example, the one who, amused at the bridal couple, "winked at himself in one of the numerous mirrors." (223)

Cultural critics thus search out the codes that inform behaviour.

A simple gesture like "winking" can become the focus for what cultural critic and anthropologist Clifford Geertz calls "thick description." Here's Geertz on "winking" (watch how he explores his subject from multiple perspectives):

> Consider ... two boys rapidly contracting the eyelids of their right eyes. In one, this is an involuntary twitch; in the other, a conspiratorial signal to a friend. The two movements are, as movements, identical; from an I-am-a-camera, "phenomenalistic" observation of them alone, one could not tell which was twitch and which was wink, or indeed whether both or either was twitch or wink. Yet the difference, however unphotographable, between a twitch and a wink is vast; as anyone unfortunate enough to have had the first taken for the second knows.... Contracting your eyelids on purpose when there exists a public code in which so doing counts as a conspiratorial signal is winking. That's all there is to it: a speck of behavior, a fleck of culture, and—*voilà!*—a gesture.
>
> That, however, is just the beginning. Suppose ... there is a third boy, who, "to give malicious amusement to his cronies," parodies the first boy's wink, as amateurish, clumsy, obvious, and so on. He, of course, does this in the same way the second boy winked and the first twitched: by contracting his right eyelids. Only this boy is neither winking nor twitching; he is

parodying someone else's, as he takes it, laughable, attempt at winking. Here, too, a socially established code exists (he will "wink" laboriously, over obviously, perhaps adding a grimace—the usual artifices of the clown); and so also does a message. Only now it is not conspiracy but ridicule that is in air. If the others think he is actually winking, his whole project misfires as completely, though with somewhat different results, as if they think he is twitching. One can go further: uncertain of his mimicking abilities, the would-be satirist may practice at home before the mirror, in which case he is not twitching, winking, or parodying, but rehearsing; though so far as what a camera ... would record he is just rapidly contracting his right eyelids like all the others. Complexities are possible, if not practically without end, at least logically so. The original winker might, for example, actually have been fake-winking, say, to mislead outsiders into imagining there was a conspiracy afoot when there in fact was not, in which case our descriptions of what the parodist is parodying and the rehearser rehearsing of course shift accordingly. (6–7)

This is a classic (some might say, "extreme") example of "saying a lot about a little." Geertz's amusing description—what he terms "a stratified hierarchy of meaningful structures in terms of which twitches, winks, fake-winks, parodies, rehearsals of parodies are produced, perceived, and interpreted"—outlines a *cultural category* used by anthropologists and critics alike. Such categories help frame (and complicate) issues, making otherwise "innocent" scenes (like the one in Crane's "The Bride") stand out and gain significance. Human behaviours and motives are complex matters; the cultural critic is intent on unpacking the layers of complexity, using thick description as a way to contextualize his or her interpretation—to understand the mirror scene as a "paradigmatic" element both of the text and of culture generally.

As a method, cultural criticism hinges on asking different questions of the text from, say, those the New Critic might ask. To understand literature culturally, you begin by looking at the scene closely, considering it from *multiple perspectives*, asking how the words, patterns, or actions are tied to power relations. Ask whose agenda is being served. What world view is being advanced? Whose aspirations or opportunities are affected? What implicit ideologies are in play or conflict? Which cultural categories does the scene fit or transgress?

Answers to these questions might prompt you to explore the nature of humour in the story—of how humour is used to oppress and repress. You might also wish to explore the *theatrical* quality of the scene, mindful of the other "stage" metaphors in the story. And what about the role of the mirrors in an environment where interior self-reflection might be assumed to be the exception rather than the rule? Critic Milne Holton notes the "curiously reflexive quality" of Potter's thoughts. The "dazzling fittings," the "darkly brilliant wood," the steel buttons of his bride's dress, the "numerous mirrors," the sardonically observant fellow passenger, the porter and the waiters: all these images, says Holton, depict "a grotesque rendering of the peculiarly reflexive quality of the modern condition" (228). In other words, Potter's thought patterns are changing; he has become a victim of the modern condition.

For a student example of cultural criticism in action, see Lydia Marston's essay in the next chapter. See how she begins with a single word ("maroon"), thinks about the word and its connotations from multiple perspectives, and then moves from a formalist focus to a cultural stance. Literary critics Katherine Sutherland and Harold Kolb, Jr. offer two further examples employing aspects of a similar critical approach.

Finding a Place for Your Interpretation in the Critical Conversation

Once you've worked out your interpretation, you need to find a place for it in the critical conversation. The student critic need not be as concerned as the professional critic about discovering *everything* that's been written on the topic—but some concern is warranted. Janet Giltrow calls this research process "identifying a knowledge deficit" and sees it as an integral feature of academic writing.

She likens the publication of professional essays to "mapping a set of positions" among those who have produced knowledge on any given topic: "On this map, no spot can be occupied simultaneously by more than one publication: that is, the publication must be 'original.' Some disciplinary locations on the map are very heavily populated. In these locations, you will find the majority of scholars working. Competition for space is keen, and researchers vie for position" (286).

According to Giltrow, there are three important ways to get your work noticed:

1. by adding to existing knowledge with new data or further reasoning

2. by identifying an area that has gone unnoticed

3. by showing that an existing position or interpretation is faulty

Some attention to what others have said should let you know when you are on the right track—when you are *asking the right kind of questions*.

Exercises

Field Stance

1. Try using the *topoi* to generate an essay. Take one of the "disturbing moments" you identified in Chapter 1 (a key word, or scene, or action, etc., that seemed out of place) and consider it in terms of the six *topoi*. Make six headings in your response journal, one for each *topos*, and then jot down how your disturbing moment relates to the story's theme (*contemptus mundi* and complexity); to any patterns of duality in the story (appearance/reality); to other similar images, scenes, actions (everywhereness); to a similar pattern in the real world (paradigm); and to any pattern of contradiction (paradox). Read over your notes and use them to write a sample opening paragraph.

2. Now take that same moment and consider it from at least two different critical perspectives. Which critical approach works best? In your response journal, begin a draft of your essay. Discuss the draft with your instructor.

CHAPTER 4

Model Essays

Student Essays

The following essay represents an exemplary piece of first-year writing. The year this essay was written, Michelle Demers won the award as top freshman English student at the University of Alberta. A panel of three professors judged this essay (and her other work) as "clearly excellent."

Stephen Crane's "The Bride Comes to Yellow Sky": Characters Moving in and out of Fashion

Michelle Demers

Written in 1898, Stephen Crane's "The Bride Comes to Yellow Sky" reflects his observations of the American West during that period: a tradition dying at the hands of Eastern influence and progress. At first glance, "The Bride" appears to be just another Western: protagonist marshal versus antagonist gun-slinging hooligan. Through subtle use of imagery, however, Crane transforms a simple Western into an analogy for an entire era and its death at the hands of change.

The changes brought by the East, historically, took many forms, not the least of which was cultural. Culture—the books read, the music played, the clothes worn, etc.—reflect the tastes and attitudes of a given era. Crane uses an image of culture—in this case, the clothing of his characters—to illustrate the infiltration of the West by Eastern ideas.

The story begins with the central character, Marshal Jack Potter, and his wife returning from their recent marriage in San Antonio, a city east of Yellow Sky. The "great Pullman" represents the East, and as it travels westward "the plains of Texas [are] pouring eastward ... sweeping over the horizon, a precipice" (377). The train (East) appears to be devouring the plains (West), and the fact that Potter and his bride are passengers on this train seems at first to indicate they are at home in this Eastern setting. As the story progresses, though, we come to realize—through their clothing—that Potter and his bride are not representative of the East, but rather of the West in transition.

Although from the West, both Potter and his bride dress in modern, Eastern clothing: he in a black suit and she in a "dress of blue cashmere" (377): Potter often looks "respectfully at his attire" (377), but the narrator also tells us that "a direct result of [Potter's] new black clothes [is] that his brick-colored hands [are] constantly performing in a most conscious fashion," and that the "glances he [devotes] to other passengers [are] furtive and shy" (377–78). Potter, who is otherwise a man "known, liked, and feared in *his* corner" (378; emphasis added), is clearly uncomfortable in this corner and in these clothes. Crane uses the word "new" to tell us it is not the fit of the clothing but, rather, the style that is causing Potter's distress.

This distress is clearly shared by his bride, who "continually [twists] her head to regard her puff sleeves" (377). Her clothing embarrasses her, and causes her to blush under "the careless scrutiny of some passengers" (377). Again we know this is not normally the case, for the narrator tells us her embarrassment is "strange to see" (377) upon her face.

Of particular interest is the bride's dress itself, and the way the narrator describes it. The dress is made of cashmere—an expensive fabric—yet the bride is described as "underclass" (377), suggesting her choice is inappropriate. The dress has "small reservations of velvet here and there" (377). "Reservations," in the literal sense, means "an expressed or tacit limitation or exception made with regard to some thing" (*OED*). The description suggests, then, that the bride carries some reservations about the changes taking place both in her life and, more subtly, in the West itself. She may be questioning her role in these changes. The dress also has "steel buttons abounding," and sleeves "very stiff, straight, and high" (377). Both suggest a certain strength and rigidity. These descriptions, coupled with her "placid, almost emotionless" (377) face, tells us the rigidity is in her attitude.

In contrast to the pair, the Negro waiters in the dining-car are dressed in "glowing white suits." They survey the Potters "with the interest and also the equanimity of men who [had] been forewarned." The waiter who serves them does so with "benevolence," an attitude of charity rather than respect (378).

Yet, despite all this, the Potters consider the East to be "the environment of their new estate" (377), and they "speedily [forget]" (378) the condescending stares of the other passengers. We know, then, that their discomfort will be temporary; that given time, their new clothes—and the new attitudes—will suit them well enough.

In Part III of the story, the narrator introduces us to the character of Scratchy Wilson, "the last one of the old gang" (382) of Yellow Sky. He is dressed in a Western shirt which has been made, ironically, "by some Jewish women on the East Side of New York" (382). His boots as well are from the East: the narrator describes them as "of the kind beloved by little sledding boys on the hillsides of New England" (382). Scratchy is accessorized by two "long, heavy" (382) revolvers.

Like his description of Potter and the bride, the narrator uses images of clothing to characterize Scratchy Wilson. The shirt is "maroon-colored" (382), which, according to contemporary notions of colour theory, suggests "pre-adolescent immaturity carried forward into adult life"; as well, it suggests a tendency "to be unrealistic and [to] have difficulty in distinguishing the practical from the visionary" (Lüscher 77). That the shirt was "purchased for the purpose of decoration" emphasizes this impracticality. The shirt is a key register of Scratchy's personality; indeed, when he meets head on with Potter in Part IV, Scratchy is referred to not by name, but again as the "man in a maroon-colored shirt" (383). This old gunslinger's choice of clothes makes him seem vaguely comic, even childlike. (Remember that his boots are beloved not by other adults, but "by little sledding boys.") All in all, Scratchy's clothing tells us he is still a child, that he has not grown with the changes and thus does not wear the new fashions well. As a result he remains isolated: the "small thing in the middle of the street" (382). His clothing also tells us that the changes brought by the East are often very subtle; as such they are able to penetrate even the staunchest opposition.

The image of the gun, Scratchy's fashion accessory, also bears comment. The gun, the symbol of the West, is, in Scratchy's hand, "long" and "heavy," suggesting a burden. Marshal Potter leaves his gun behind in Yellow Sky when he travels east to San Anton', a gesture that seems incomprehensible to Scratchy: "Don't tell me no lie like that," he says. "There ain't a man in Texas ever seen you without no gun" (384). When the two finally meet in the challenge of East versus West, Scratchy's revolver "[drops] to his side" (384) in defeat.

We have seen, then, how Crane uses the imagery of clothing to portray a culture in transition. From the shiny suits of the Eastern waiters, to the awkward—but nevertheless Eastern—wedding clothes of the Potters, and down to the adolescent Western clothing of Scratchy Wilson, Crane's narrator highlights references to fashion and provides a subtle index regarding which characters are in or out of style. To some extent, of course, each character feels out of place, caught within the tension between old and new, between Western and Eastern values.

Works Cited

Crane, Stephen. "The Bride Comes to Yellow Sky." *McClure's Magazine* 10 (February 1898): 377–84. Print.

Lüscher, Max. *The Lüscher Color Test*. Trans. Ian Scott. New York: Washington Square P, 1969. Print.

Some Points to Consider

- What is the most impressive aspect of this essay? Do you notice how the author says a lot about a little?

- Demers writes very well. Which phrases in particular demonstrate critical confidence and style?

- Could the introduction have done more to contextualize the critical issue?

- Where are quotations used especially well? Are there points where a paraphrase, instead of direct quotation, might have worked better? Does the author need to place the page number after each quotation?

- Which critical approach has she used? Has it been used consistently throughout the essay?

- Which of the six key critical *topoi* does Demers employ here?

- What does the reference to Lüscher's colour theory add to Demers's reading? Are there ways that she might have developed Lüscher's schema even further?

The next essay was written by Ryan Miller, a student who has carried on with graduate studies in English.

The "Weary Gentlemen" of Yellow Sky:
Implosion, Silence, and Quiet Acceptance

Ryan Miller

Throughout Stephen Crane's "The Bride Comes to Yellow Sky," one notices that despite the charged overtones of Western genre, much of the short story is spent calmly, "like a man waiting in a barber shop" (377). Rather than a continuous upsurge of energy, the progression of events moves with an undeniable sense of slowness and trepidation when compared to the introduction of the speeding train and its "dignity of motion" (377). Moreover, the distance we are told this "Pullman" will cross in its "thousand miles" (377) is alien in terms of its scope, and worlds removed from any expanse, social or otherwise, traversed elsewhere in the story. In many ways, the references to its distinction accurately reflect its purpose: the "pulling" of "man" towards the apex of his individual and collective destiny. It is, after all, primarily men who are affected in the story. The only woman, Jack Potter's bride, possesses an optimism about the future not seen anywhere else, as though it is only the social role of men that is about to change. If so, those in Yellow Sky represent the rails yet untouched. In the face of a change they know will arrive, they can do little but resign themselves to moments of quiet acceptance, mourning what will soon become a loss of the old world. What results is a town filled with "periods of stillness" and "immovable silence" (381). The train's intention to keep its schedule suggests that this passing, if nothing else, is inevitable. Endings will simply come, and by their own definitive nature, cannot be stopped or slowed.

The weariness and lethargy of the men in Yellow Sky is found in many places, and although the town in general is described as "dozing," this slumber is evident in no better place than the "Weary Gentleman" saloon. Here, the building's name essentially speaks for itself. It is both a gathering place for those who have come to accept their fate, and a sanctuary against those like Scratchy Wilson who still resist. Inside, there is a tremendous lack of energy, and in broader terms, a sense of implosion—as if any energy that is present is being swallowed. It does not exude a bright and lively atmosphere as one might expect, but rather, a "chapel-like gloom" (380) normally reserved for funerals. In many ways, these people already feel the end of who they are. We are told, for instance, that the Texans inside "did not care to talk at that time," while others in the saloon "did not talk as a general practice" (380). The absence of voice, or the willingness to use it, is significant: it suggests a similar absence of identity parallel to the silence that is created. It is as though they have already accepted that nothing spoken will change the course of events. Indeed, much of the silence present in "The Bride" seems designed for the characters' contemplation of their future roles, not to mention the reflection upon old ones.

Any voices which do appear quickly diminish to "mere whisperings" (381). This is in stark contrast to the "terrible invitations" (382) of Scratchy Wilson, who regards the "surrounding stillness [as forming] the arch of a tomb over him" (382). In fact, the only person who actually uses his voice to any civilized extent in Yellow Sky is the drummer, an Eastern salesman who observes events with the "interest of a foreigner" (381). His sales pitch brings both goods and the good news of progress. He is not one to sympathize with or understand Scratchy's resistance, for he himself is a man comfortable with his Eastern role.

Scratchy Wilson is backed against the wall. His outrage is explained in terms of a drunken stupor, but on another level it represents his fears about a future role which is uncertain. At one point in the story, he regards the closed door of the "Weary Gentleman" saloon and demands to be let in. Inwardly, he desires to be calm and collected like those inside, but he leaves angered because of his helplessness and isolation. One could even argue that he is searching to lose a gun battle with Jack Potter, and as a result, burn, rather than fade, out of existence. His is the only true action in the short story. However, like everything else, the energy of whatever moment is there eventually disappears, as he is pulled down in the funnel of the story's hourglass nature.

Aside from the characters and setting, the lack of energy in Crane's short story is reflected in the climax of the plot, or as one could argue, the lack thereof. Drawn to the conclusion, one is expecting the rise of Scratchy's rampage to be answered or fulfilled with some form of dramatic release. However, this does not occur. Instead, when faced with the fact that his most "ancient antagonist" (382) has moved on into a new time and a new era, Scratchy is reluctantly forced to do the same. The sudden loss, or implosion, of the energy that was momentarily present within the narrative reflects what occurs throughout much of the story: something large and loud one moment becomes disturbingly quiet the next, demonstrating the temporal uncertainties faced in everyday life. Stephen Crane uses this lack of energy in the story to show how old voices can be stilled as easily as stillness can give voice to quiet change. The process of accepting this passage from one to the other is key to finding a place in the world.

Works Cited

Crane, Stephen. "The Bride Comes to Yellow Sky." *McClure's Magazine* 10 (February 1898): 377–84. Print.

Some Points to Consider

- What is the most impressive aspect of Ryan Miller's essay? How does its approach differ from that of Michelle Demers?

- Do you notice any differences in vocabulary or phrasing between the two essays?

- The author does not state his thesis explicitly in his opening paragraph. Does this strategy work well?

- Which of the six *topoi* does the writer emphasize in his interpretation?

- The essay's subject, "an implosion of energy," seems to lend itself to a deconstructive approach. How would you develop the interpretation along these lines?

- Do you notice the impressive use of the paradox *topos* in the final paragraph?

The final student essay was written by Lydia Marston for a third-year criticism seminar. Like the other student critics, Marston has received both general praise and awards for her writing.

Marooned and Gilded: The Iconography of Scratchy Wilson in Stephen Crane's "The Bride Comes to Yellow Sky"

Lydia Marston

In "The Bride Comes to Yellow Sky," Stephen Crane navigates the theme of the wild, untamed West surrounded and lost in the tide of change "pouring" (377) in from the East. Crane's character "Scratchy Wilson" embodies the shipwrecked youth of the West; he is "a simple child of the earlier plains" (384)—an innocent in the vast sea of grass, "a thousand miles from one end ... to the other" (377), that is Texas. With an impressionistic daub of "red" colour here and a "gilded" historical metaphor there, Crane weaves a verbal texture supporting the theme of change. In Crane's deft iconography, the very materials of Scratchy's clothing are used to explore his identity. Scratchy's "maroon-colored flannel shirt," and "his boots [with] red tops [and] gilded imprints" (382), for example, are key images in Crane's 1898 construction. More than an exotic colour, "maroon" is symbolic of someone abandoned on a desolate island or coast—in this case, marooned on the coastline of the frontier town called Yellow Sky. Scratchy is a man left alone, "the last one of the old gang that used to hang out along the river" (382). When drunk, Scratchy abandons the civilized world altogether, quixotically "challeng[ing] ... the surrounding stillness ... of a deserted village" (382)—his "semblance" of a desolate island in the sea of change.

The subtle, and occasionally even bold, references to the sea and to ships found in "The Bride Comes to Yellow Sky" seem anomalous without the "maroon" key that is Scratchy's shirt. In sharp contrast to the simple "new black clothes" worn by Potter, and the "dress of blue" (377) worn by the bride, Crane intends us to see the strangely specific colour "maroon" as highly significant. Equally significant and anomalous are Scratchy's "red ... gilded" boots, which carry us, like mythic seven league boots, to "New England ... hillsides" as foreign to Texas as "winter" and "little sledding boys" (382). This intrusion of "England," the original colonizer, into a scene where the "maroon shirt" has been identified as an import from "the East Side of New

York" (382), the busiest port of entry in America, underscores the invasiveness of Eastern expansion. Scratchy and the West, associated with the spontaneity of a primitive South Sea island, are already marooned and marginalized by a "traitor to the feelings of Yellow Sky" (379), with only "the keening Rio Grande" (378) bearing witness.

Crane's repeated detailing of Scratchy, in both Parts III and IV of the story, as "a man in a maroon ... shirt" is intended to draw our attention to this word's importance; it is a link to his other nautical references. These references begin when Scratchy's nemesis, Sheriff Potter, rides "over the horizon" in a "great Pullman" bearing a marked resemblance to an ocean liner—with its "dignity of motion," its "brass," its "sea-green figured velvet" (377) and its dark wood. Moreover, a waiter on board is said to "steer Potter and his bride through their meal" the way "a fatherly pilot" (378) would take a ship to safe harbour. Later, when Scratchy's rampage is announced, the barkeeper in Yellow Sky is made to confirm the ship-like imagery by wishing that Potter "would sail in and pull the kinks out of this thing" (382). As though battening down the hatches for Scratchy's stormy passage, the barkeeper then "lock[s] and bar[s]" the door and "pull[s] in [the] heavy wooden shutters" (380).

A stormy passage also awaits the bride. She shares with Scratchy images of ships, distant shores and drowning. Her dress is blue as water and has foreign fabrics—"cashmere" wool and "velvet" (377)— imported across oceans from exotic places. Her face, which turns "yellow as old cloth" (383) on encountering Scratchy and his deadly guns, is the colour of old sails, an image conjured when she and Potter walk as though "bowed against a strong wind" (383). When Scratchy recognizes "the drooping, drowning woman" as Potter's bride, he is "like a creature allowed a glimpse of another world" (384). Marriage, the "foreign condition" (384) he encounters, is only another manifestation of this strange new place in which he finds himself marooned, uncomprehending and unable to fight the tide of change. Scratchy's "low collar," from which the "cords of his neck straighten and [sink], straighten and [sink]" (382), show him as a man barely able to keep his head above the water of this new era.

In case we did not grasp the significance of his allusions to ships and the sea by the end of his story, Crane gives us one more descriptive clue, as incongruously and pointedly at odds with his setting in hot, landlocked Yellow Sky as the reference to "little sledding boys." He leaves us with the picture of Scratchy, in his "maroon" shirt and his "gilded" red boots, holstering his "starboard revolver" and walking away alone, leaving "funnel-shaped tracks in the heavy sand" (384) of a desert island shore in the middle of Texas.

While the "maroon" shirt sails us to distant shores, the "gilded" boots turn our footsteps to the heart of America. With this one word Crane invokes an era marked, "historically," by the most "unconquerable kind of snobbery" (378), an era whose name was coined with the 1873 publication of Mark Twain and Charles Dudley Warner's novel, *The Gilded Age*. Marked by rapid national economic expansion, wealth, and fashionable superficiality as "stiff, straight, and high" as the empty "puff sleeves" that so "embarrass" (377) the bride, the "Gilded Age" brought with it a unity of ideology which left no room for dissenting voices. Crane makes it clear that voices like Scratchy's do not have the power to communicate: their language is obsolete, their "cries of ferocious challenge [ring] against walls of silence" (382).

To show how it feels to be in Scratchy's "boots," Crane modifies the "voice" which describes his character in Part III, his "rampage" (382) scene. Scratchy "yell[s] ... shrilly ... in a volume that seem[s] to have no relation to the ordinary vocal strength of man," he "roar[s] ... terrible invitations," he "bellow[s] and fume[s] and howl[s]" (382); but we do not hear him. His "chanting [of] Apache scalp music" (382) removes him from modern culture, makes him a thing of the past, like the Indian warrior: incomprehensible. Crane encloses him in "the arch of a tomb" (382) formed by his reportage, surrounds him with "walls of silence," and never allows his readers to hear Scratchy's actual words "quoted."

It is only in Part IV, when he comes in contact with Potter, that we hear Scratchy's voice. He has become a silenced thing existing only in the world of an "other," of Potter, who in his funereal "new black clothes" brings an advancing civilization (a "foreign condition") which sweeps Texas, and Scratchy, "into the east" over "a precipice" (377). The Pullman, which "prove[s]" that the "vast flats" of Texas are "pouring eastward" (377), has "dazzling fittings" of "shining brass" which mimic the brass-coloured gilding on Scratchy's boots. While the train "reflect[s]" the "environment of [a] new estate" (377), Scratchy's boots only leave "funnel-shaped tracks" in shifting sand. The "precipice," over which Texas is swept, is a counterpoint to the "hillsides of New England" where Scratchy's "gilded ... red" boots take him. These "hillsides" are tame, civilized slopes. They represent a slippery slide into the "Gilded Age," and a new order as implacable as gravity, as certain as "winter" (382), the season of endings.

Gilding is purely for decoration, and we are told that Scratchy's shirt is also "for purposes of decoration" (382). This symmetry of purpose makes it clear that Scratchy does not fit into the product-oriented, work-driven society "sweeping" in to surround him. Most of the other characters in Crane's story are defined by work: the "porter," the "waiter," the "barkeeper," the "drummer," the "bride," and the "sheriff," but Scratchy is associated with play: like "little sledding boys," he'll "play ... in a musician's way" with his guns and with the "town [which is] a toy for him" (382). His pathos is that he is "a simple child of the earlier plains" (384). He does not fit into the "foreign condition" that the annexation of Texas (the only state once an independent nation) brings to Yellow Sky.

Scratchy's "cries of ferocious challenge" against psychic annexation are connected to his "boots [with] red tops" through the grammatically incongruous "And" in the opening paragraph of Part III. A further connection is then made with Potter who meets this challenge, and whose "brick red hands" (377) identify him as an active participant in the construction of a "new," controlled, urban state. His "bricks" are the building blocks of a civilization, the "great stone god" (382) which excludes characters like Scratchy behind "walls of silence." The connection between these two men is emphasized by the colour red—found not only in their boots and hands but in their faces. In Part I we are told that Potter's "face [is] reddened from ... the wind and sun" (377) and later in the story Scratchy's "face flames" and is "livid" from frustration and "whisky" (382–84). Crane has Scratchy move "a pace backward" in his red boots but Potter's heels do not move "an inch backward" (384). Potter wins "with no offer of fight" (382) because he brings "the foreign condition" against which ordinary "weapons," like "revolvers," hold no currency.

Crane's currency of language in "The Bride Comes to Yellow Sky" is not at all like the "fumbled out ... coin" (379) Potter gives the porter at the end of Part I. Each of Crane's "coins" is carefully chosen and precisely placed in his short story's construction. The seeming incongruity of "gilded red" boots and "maroon" shirt is like the "X marks the spot" of a treasure map, elegantly drawn to lead us to a "maroon[ed]" man fighting a last, futile battle against "the environment of the new estate." Crane's impressionistically placed colours lead our mind's eye from one image clue to another. We, like Scratchy, become "creature[s] allowed a glimpse of another world" (384).

Works Cited

Crane, Stephen. "The Bride Comes to Yellow Sky." *McClure's Magazine* 10 (February 1898): 377–84. Print.

Some Points to Consider

- What aspects of the writing distinguish this essay as senior-level work?

- Is the author's use of nautical metaphors in her opening paragraph effective?

- How does she contextualize her focus on the word "maroon"?

- Which of the six *topoi* does this essay emphasize? Is there something in her critical method that allowed Marston to discover so original an interpretation? (In over 100 years of critical discussion, no other critic had commented on Scratchy Wilson as a "marooned" figure.)

- Marston integrates textual evidence throughout her essay. No claim or observation lacks detailed support. Are there places, however, where she might have limited the number of quotations cited? Is it necessary to put quotation marks around single words like "winter" and "coins"?

- Another impressive aspect of the essay is its use of the paradigm *topos* (the New Historicist gesture), which complements the close reading of textual patterns found *in* the text. What does the commentary on the "Gilded Age" add to her interpretation?

- Both Miller and Marston discuss silences and voice. Compare their interpretations: which do you prefer?

Professional Essays

The first example of professional writing is from Alice Farley, former chair of English at Southern Illinois University at Edwardsville. The essay was originally published as a "critical note" in The Explicator 42 *(Fall 1983): 45–47. Farley's remarkably concise explication offers a model of close reading and suggests the power and utility of the short critical essay.*

Crane's "The Bride Comes to Yellow Sky"

Alice Farley (a.k.a. Alice Hall Petry)

Insufficient attention has been paid to Stephen Crane's use of names in his fiction. That this particular aspect of his literary style is worthy of interest has been suggested by John Berryman, who in 1950 noted that Crane "could be adroit on occasion with names" and that he "was alive to weird names, names that invite query and ridicule" (309, 240). Working within this vein, Donald B. Gibson has argued that the name of the character "John Twelve" in *The Monster* evidently was designed to send the discerning reader to Chapter 12 of the Gospel according to St. John—a chapter which contains the story of Lazarus and thereby underscores the Christlike aspects of Dr. Trescott (see Gibson 137). But this sort of inquiry proves fruitful not only with unusual names such as "John Twelve": even Crane's tendency to employ "the commonest possible" names and, for that matter, his "compulsive namelessness" (Berryman 310–11) are more significant than one might assume. For example, a consideration of "The Bride Comes to Yellow Sky" shows that Crane chose names ideally suited to the revelation of his characters' personalities and situations, to the development of the story's theme, and to the setting of tone.

As the characters of his "hilariously funny parody of neoromantic lamentations over 'The Passing of the West'" (Cady 103), Crane provides us with an anonymous bride, a marshal named Jack Potter, and one Scratchy Wilson, the local hell-raiser. In his depiction of the meeting of these three characters in a single anti-climactic scene, Crane is dramatizing the dying of the sentimentalized West with the encroachment of the lifestyle of the civilized East; and nothing better illustrates this rather abstract cultural and demographic concept than his refusal to give Jack Potter's new bride a name. As an individual she is insignificant. She matters only as a representative of the new Eastern order, and to underscore her symbolic status Crane depersonalizes her in the most obvious way: anonymity. Scratchy must be stopped dead in his tracks not by the individual—"The Bride was not pretty, nor was she very young" (377)—but by his recognition of the changes in the social order which she represents and, concomitantly, of the imminent death of an already-passing way of life which Scratchy represents.

Although the bride is given only a generic name, her husband is given a specific and seemingly common one, Jack Potter; but in fact Crane chose it for its uncommon capacity to express the marshal's personality and situation, as well as to help convey the theme and tone of the tale. The very blandness of his name stands in immediate contrast to what one would expect of a Texas marshal. By the 1890s, dead or retired were the marshals with such colourful names as Wyatt Earp, Wild Bill Hickok, and Bat Masterson, and with them had died the romantic notion of Boot Hill, the traditional final resting-place of desperadoes and macho marshals. In its place, Crane has subtly substituted a far less appealing entity: the surname "Potter" suggests a "Potter's Field," traditionally a graveyard for the homeless and friendless. As the ranking leader of the Yellow Sky community, Marshal Potter controls it virtually as his domain; indeed, Crane states explicitly that he was "a man known, liked, and feared in his corner, a prominent person" (378). Ultimately the entire town of Yellow Sky—a name indicative of sunsets and death—is one huge cemetery for the dying Westerners: it is, in fine, "Marshal Potter's 'field.'"

That Potter functions less as a macho marshal than as the caretaker of a town rapidly turning into a graveyard is also conveyed by other connotations of his name. Far from being routinely well-groomed *à la* Earp or Masterson, Potter is so embarrassed by his "new black clothes" (a rather funereal note) that "his brick-colored hands were constantly performing in a most conscious fashion" (377). The surname Potter denotes, of course, one who works with clay, and it is typical of the rich diction of Crane's best fiction that this "potter" has brick-colored hands and lives in an adobe house. His essential earthiness is far more suggestive of a grave-digger or farmer (in nineteenth-century slang, to "plant" someone is to bury him) than of a slick Western marshal. As a final meaning of his name, Jack Potter is a "Jackpot-er"—the "jackpot" being the bride; but in keeping with the ironic, debunking tone of the story, she is far less appealing than one might expect of the woman "won" by a Western marshal: with her "steel buttons abounding" and "plain, under-class countenance," she "had cooked, and … expected to cook, dutifully" (377).

Just as complex as the name of Jack Potter is that of his "ancient antagonist," Scratchy Wilson (382). As George Monteiro has argued, the action in "The Bride" may be interpreted as a type of Saturnalia, with Scratchy as a demonic figure, what with his "maroon-colored" shirt, red-topped boots, and face "flamed in a rage begot of whisky" (382). His name, too, connotes the demonic, for "Old Scratch" is a traditional nickname for the devil. The "y" suffix of "Scratchy," however, nicely deflates Wilson's demonism, his capacity to do real harm—and his harmlessness is in keeping not only with the idea of a Saturnalia (which is ritualized behaviour), but also with the systematic debunking of the West which the story achieves. After all, when sober Scratchy is "'all right—kind of simple—wouldn't hurt a fly—nicest fellow in town'" (382). In fine, his status as the meanest hombre in Yellow Sky belies his actual personality: Scratchy is less brave than pot-valiant ("scratched," in fact, is slang for "tipsy"), and as such his reputation as a Western bad-man merely "scratches the surface" of Wilson. Furthermore, the word "scratchy" signifies both "irritating" and "irritable": the townspeople find his periodic rampages annoying (in the "Weary Gentleman" saloon, only the "drummer," an out-of-towner, is genuinely excited), and the drunk and frustrated Wilson yells at the sky, shoots at a piece of paper, and roars "menacing information" to the unresponsive town "as it occur[s] to him" (382). This "small thing in the middle of the street" flies into an impotent rage because "There was no offer of fight; no offer of fight"; even the "calm adobes preserved their demeanor" (382). It is perhaps significant in this regard that one slang definition of a "scratch" is "An unknown, insignificant, or chronically poor person, one who is to be ignored" (Wentworth and Flexner 450–51)—as, indeed, the towns-people of Yellow Sky tend to perceive Wilson. Finally, to "scratch" also means to withdraw from a contest. With the words "'I s'pose it's all off now'" (384), Wilson signifies his decision to withdraw from a gunfight with Jack Potter and in so doing to decline engaging in any active resistance to the encroachment of the East.

It is well within reason to assume that Crane was aware of the myriad implications of names he chose for the three characters of "The Bride Comes to Yellow Sky." As a poet, Crane was peculiarly sensitive to the dense web of connotative and denotative meanings which could be conveyed with a well-chosen word; and, as Berryman and Gibson have recognized, this sensitivity could also be brought to bear upon his choice of fictional names.[1]

| 83 |

---

1. Throughout this essay, my sources of information on slang have been Wentworth and Flexner, plus Eric Partridge.

Works Cited

Berryman, John. *Stephen Crane.* New York: William Sloane Associates, 1950. Print.

Cady, Edwin H. *Stephen Crane.* Rev. ed. Boston: Twayne Publishers, 1980. Print.

Gibson, Donald B. *The Fiction of Stephen Crane.* Carbondale and Edwardsville: Southern Illinois UP, 1968. Print.

Monteiro, George. "Stephen Crane's 'The Bride Comes to Yellow Sky.'" *Approaches to the Short Story.* Ed. Neil D. Isaacs and Louis H. Leiter. San Francisco: Chandler, 1963. 221–37. Print.

Partridge, Eric. *A Dictionary of Slang and Unconventional English.* 7th ed. New York: Macmillan, 1970. Print.

Wentworth, Harold, and Stuart Berg Flexner, eds. *Dictionary of American Slang.* New York: Thomas Y. Crowell, 1960. Print.

Some Points to Consider

- What is the most impressive aspect of Farley's essay? As with Demers's essay, do you notice how Farley says a lot about a little?

- Since both Demers and Farley use the same critical approach—they trace the significance of a single textual pattern—it seems worth comparing the two essays. As a professional critic Farley works hard to establish not just a "reading" but also a "critical issue." How does she do this? How does she situate her reading as part of an ongoing critical conversation? What is the function of phrases such as "indeed," "in fine," "after all," and "of course"?

- Look especially at how Farley uses transitions to link ideas. Can you identify two or three linking devices?

- What is the function of the secondary sources cited by Farley?

- Where are quotations used especially well? How does Farley use quotations from Crane's text?

- Since she is writing a very brief essay (as required by *The Explicator*, which publishes only short essays), Farley must condense a lot of information into a relatively small space. She doesn't have room to develop a long argument. Does the essay fulfill its announced purpose: to show that Crane's use of names helps reveal character, supports the story's theme, and sets the story's tone?

- Which of the six key critical *topoi* does Farley employ here?

- Why is it important that Crane displays a poetic sensibility to connotative and denotative meanings? Can you find other examples where Crane's choice of words adds to our pleasure and understanding of the story?

The second professional essay is by Katherine Sutherland, Associate Professor of English at Thompson Rivers University. Professor Sutherland's reading joins the appearance/reality topos with the paradigm orientation of feminist criticism.

"Never the Twain Shall Meet"

Katherine Sutherland

My father has always had a weakness for bad jokes, and one that he told me when I was a kid goes like this: If east is east and west is west, and never the twain shall meet, where's the twain? Answer: on the twacks. The punch-line is obviously silly, but the question posed by the joke reflects a particularly entrenched North American belief about nation and region—or, more aptly, nation versus region. In both Canada and the United States, mythologies of nationality are partly formed through notions of region; though the U.S. is sometimes grandly divided into the North and the South, it is also divided equally often (and equally grandly) into East and West, as is Canada. Indeed, glorified historical constructions of the "West" as both a region and state of mind, which can be equated variously with freedom, hardiness, and lawlessness, are commonplace in North American literature and are implicated in the ideology of "the American Dream."

This East/West dichotomy is a clear point of reference in Stephen Crane's "The Bride Comes to Yellow Sky," as many critics have observed. Milne Holton writes, for instance, that "'The Bride

Comes to Yellow Sky' is a story of two kinds of orders—of two American civilizations—one of the East and the city, whose collective imagination is dedicated to machines, manufactured objects, and institutions; the other the West of the frontier town, its communal imagination dominated by Nature, animals, and individual violence" (227). Marston LaFrance argues that within the story "the images of the East suggest a more mature social reality than ritual gunfighting, and Yellow Sky in the course of the story becomes socially more mature" (213). These interpretations of Crane's story are valid in their collective assertion that the East is associated with social order while the West, represented by the town of Yellow Sky, signifies disorder—a disorder, however, that is rapidly being replaced by an invading, officious East: "with the coming of the railroad, the nomadic, independent, heroic conditions of existence of the region were fast disappearing. With the railroad came a mercantile, impersonal, interdependent civilization" (Holton 227). I would like to suggest an alternative reading of the East/ West dichotomy in "The Bride Comes to Yellow Sky," however, one in which the East is associated with women while the West is associated with men; in this analysis, the female becomes an invasive and subtly hostile force which intends to curtail the heroic and ultimately male freedoms of the West. This argument relies partly on the comparison between the bride and the Pullman coach in the story, a comparison that implicitly associates the bride with four things feared by the male characters: civilization, capitalism, castration, and death.

The opening description of the bride is obviously echoed in a later description of the Pullman coach, as the use of italics makes clear. The bride, whose nameless state lends her an allegorical status in the text, is described thus:

> The bride was not pretty, nor was she very young. She wore a dress of blue cashmere, with *small reservations of velvet* here and there and with *steel buttons* abounding. She continually twisted her head to regard her puff sleeves, very *stiff, straight, and high.* (377; emphasis added)

The coach, pointed to by the husband, Sheriff Jack Potter, a few paragraphs later, bears undeniable resemblance to the bride:

> He pointed out to her the dazzling fittings of the coach, and in truth her eyes opened wider as she contemplated the *sea-green figured velvet, the shining brass, silver, and glass*, the wood that

gleamed darkly brilliant as the surface of a pool of oil. At one end a bronze figure *sturdily* held a *support* for a separated chamber, and at convenient places on the ceiling were frescoes in olive and silver. (377; emphasis added)

Both coach and woman are fitted in velvet and metal; attention is paid to the height and substance of the woman's pose and the car in which she is posed. The luxurious appointments of the coach represent the growing domination of urban capitalism and civilization; it is ironic that these metropolitan forces are associated with women, as trains are more often symbols linked to masculinity, with their steel, tubular forward action. Here, however, the train is plush, even decadent, and linked to the bride. Jack Potter feels impotent on the train, where he is clearly out of his element, even patronized by the porter; this is only the first darkly comic reference to mock castration in the story.

There are contrasts as well between descriptions of the bride and the Pullman coach, which are worth noting: the fittings of the woman's costume are less elaborate and attractive than the "dazzling fittings" of the coach (she has only "small reservations of velvet" and "steel buttons," not "shining brass, silver and glass" trimmings), suggesting that the metaphorical association between the woman and the train is more elaborate than the simple equation of two invading forces. To be more precise, the East is associated with the train—or modern, mercantile forces—but both the East and the train are associated with women, making the train a motif of seductive opulence that is all horsehair stuffing underneath. As Chester Wolford writes, "Crane makes clear that the 'new' (Eastern society and values) that replaces the 'old' (Western society and values) is not quite the fresh, young, boundlessly hopeful generation or society usually associated with comedy" (28). David Halliburton writes that "the advent of the train is associated, as it so often was in his century, with challenge and change" (228), but while such progressive notions are usually positive values, in "The Bride Comes to Yellow Sky," the "challenge and change" represented by the bride are clearly negative values. Not only is the bride described as unattractive and "clumsy" (377) in her manner, her new husband is ashamed of her. His newly married status "weigh[s] upon him like a leaden slab" (378); he feels that he is "heinous" and has "committed an extraordinary crime" for which "his friends [will] not forgive him" (378). It is ambiguous whether the crime is to have eloped or to have married at all.

87

Arguably, this story barely masks a deeply embedded fear of female power, which is reflected in a profound suspicion of female domestication. Chester Wolford argues that

> If Potter represents the "New" West, and Scratchy the Old West, then the prefiguring at the story's beginning allows the walkdown to be thought of as a confrontation between the new "civilized" West—the railroad, law and order, and domestic institutions such as marriage—and the old "Wild" West. (30)

And, as Kenneth Bernard points out, the loss of the "Wild" West is not treated positively in the story: "Basically, it is an elegy; it laments the passing of the old West and its values and deplores the rise of the new, civilized values of the East" (435). There is only one reference to women in the story other than the bride; it occurs in the first description of Jack Potter's nemesis, Scratchy Wilson, who is wearing "a maroon-colored flannel shirt, which had been purchased for purposes of decoration and made, principally, by some Jewish women on the east side of New York" (382). Like the association between the bride and the Pullman coach, this passage links women, the East, domestication (sewing), and alien status, as registered in the vaguely anti-Semitic reference to "some Jewish women."

Ultimately, this Eastern/female presence in the story can be subtly associated with death. Kenneth Bernard explores the use of figures and rhetoric that equate the return of the married sheriff with a symbolic death:

> Wilson gets drunk, not knowing that Potter is away. He bellows and fumes and sways through the town, shooting it up, venting his rage over what is gone…. He is reliving a time now dead the only way he knows how. But it is dead. When he yells, it is "as if the surrounding stillness formed the arch of a tomb over him." Potter, whose return as a married man marks the end of homage to the myth [of the West], feels his deed weighing on him "like a leaden slab." And when he meets Wilson later and his "mouth seemed merely to be a grave for his tongue," the words have a double meaning. (436)

This analysis leaves little doubt that the story imagines a symbolic death of the rituals of the "Wild" West: the town's saloon is called the "Weary Gentleman," after all. The questions that arise, then, are what exactly has died, and what exactly has caused this death? There might be several answers to these questions, depending on the critical approach, but a feminist analysis will surely answer these questions by stating that it is male freedom and potency that have died, and women are the killers.

The story ends with a failed gunfight—and gunfights are perhaps the clearest sign of the masculine order of disorder in the mythical Wild West. The fight fails, and it fails because Potter is without a gun specifically because he has gotten married: "I ain't got a gun because I've just come from San Anton' with my wife. I'm married" (384). The obvious connection between guns and masculine potency leads to the conclusion that this scene parodies the emasculation of the male warrior through his seduction by a woman; in other words, if Mrs. Potter were to be given a name in the story, the most apt one might be Delilah. No person dies in this scene, but male pride is sacrificed on the altar of female, domestic power. It has been argued that the many references to red in the story may be associated with the blood of male violence—Milne Holton suggests that "Part of the evidence is to be found in the recurrent colours of black and red in the images of the 'red tops' of Wilson's boots, his 'maroon-colored flannel shirt,' his 'blueblack revolver' and of Potter's 'new black clothes,' 'reddened' face, and 'brick-colored hands'" (231). It is equally plausible that red and black might be associated with the blood that emerges from the "dark continent" (as Freud notoriously put it) of female sexuality. The bride is frequently described as blushing, and the "brick-colored hands" of the impotent man who is animated only through the hidden power of his wife suggests that, upon consideration, Lady Macbeth might be a more fitting literary allusion for the bride than Delilah.

Red and black are culturally linked to blood and death; the dominant sign of female sexuality is blood—the blood of menstruation, of first intercourse, and of childbirth. Female sexuality is also associated with death: birth initiates death, and the womb is linked to the tomb as a *matrix* (Latin for "womb") for the mysteries of human existence. Anthropologists have argued that taboos of menstruation, particularly prohibitions against intercourse with a menstruating woman, are linked to a fear of castration (blood on the penis) and a fear of death (Buckley and Gottlieb)—blood for women may symbolize life and power through reproduction, but for men it generally signals the loss of these things. Thus, these colours may be linked to

89

the notion of the usurpation of male power by female power, in that the power of taking life is being superseded by the power of making life—or, in symbolic terms, the blood of male violence is being stopped by the blood of female reproduction—and by extension, the reproduction of civilizing Eastern values and economic development.

Although she is never named and scarcely speaks in the story, the bride dominates the action and the plot merely through her presence: her simple appearance on the scene of the gunfight in the end not only terminates this particular confrontation, it symbolically interrupts the generic conventions of the Western itself and, by extension, the overriding myth of the West. The death of this myth is rendered in pathetic terms in "The Bride Comes to Yellow Sky," with the final image depicting a deflated Wilson as "a simple child of the earlier plains" (384)—in short, as a little boy who may be forced to grow up.

In the end, however, it is not the compromised masculinity of Potter or Wilson that moves me. Instead, I think about the nameless bride: what were her dreams? And when she married the middle-aged sheriff of a one-horse town, what adventures or myths did she abandon, the time of her life falling silently through an hourglass like "funnel-shaped tracks in the heavy sand" (384)?

Works Cited

Bernard, Kenneth. "'The Bride Comes to Yellow Sky': History as Elegy." *Stephen Crane's Career: Perspectives and Evaluations.* Ed. Thomas A. Gullason. New York: New York UP, 1972. 435–39. Print.

Buckley, Thomas, and Alma Gottlieb, eds. *Blood Magic: The Anthropology of Menstruation.* Berkeley: U of California P, 1988. Print.

Crane, Stephen. "The Bride Comes to Yellow Sky." *McClure's Magazine* 10 (February 1898): 377–84. Print.

Halliburton, David. *The Color of the Sky: A Study of Stephen Crane.* New York: Cambridge UP, 1989. Print.

Holton, Milne. *Cylinder of Vision: The Fiction and Journalistic Writing of Stephen Crane.* Baton Rouge: Louisiana State UP, 1972. Print.

LaFrance, Marston. *A Reading of Stephen Crane*. Oxford: Clarendon P, 1971. Print.

Wolford, Chester. *Stephen Crane: A Study of the Short Fiction*. Boston: Twayne Publishers, 1989. Print.

Some Points to Consider

- What is the most impressive aspect of Sutherland's essay? What does it help you see or understand differently? Do you agree with all the points she makes?

- Like Farley, Sutherland establishes both a "reading" and a "critical issue." How does she do this? How does she situate her reading as part of an ongoing critical conversation? Is the conversation she enters the same as the one implied by Farley's essay? What is the function of Sutherland's autobiographical opening?

- Farley regards the bride as an "abstract cultural and demographic concept," but "as an individual," says Farley, "she is insignificant." Sutherland, on the other hand, wonders about her dreams, her abandoned "adventures or myths." Which interpretation do you find the most persuasive? How does Sutherland make room for her feminist reading?

- How would you characterize the tone of Sutherland's critical voice? Do you find Sutherland's use of the personal pronoun "I" effective?

- Where are quotations used especially well? How does Sutherland use block quotations to make her case?

- Unlike Farley, Sutherland wrote her essay as a contribution for this book. (I asked Dr. Sutherland to write a model of the kind of paper she would like to receive from her own senior-level English students.) If she had been writing exclusively for an audience of fellow critics, how might she have changed the essay?

- As a feminist critic, Sutherland gives much more attention to the bride than we find in essays by other readers. Why would other (male and female) critics have had so little to say about the role of women in the story? How would you characterize Sutherland's feminist approach?

- Sutherland claims that the "story barely masks a deeply embedded fear of female power": who is afraid and how does this fear make itself known? Do we have evidence to suggest that Crane himself was fearful of female power and sexuality? Or was he writing a story critiquing such fear? Is Sutherland's reading "fair" to Crane's intent? Or, over 100 years ago, would Crane simply be unaware of his own prejudices and sexism?

- Which of the six key critical *topoi* does Sutherland employ here?

- Why does Sutherland make literary allusions to two other notorious figures, Delilah and Lady Macbeth?

- How does Sutherland's use of colour imagery extend (or contradict) the approaches of Michelle Demers and Lydia Marston to colour symbolism? Which of the readings do you find the most convincing?

The final professional essay, written especially for this book, is by Harold Kolb, Jr., Professor of English and American Studies at the University of Virginia. Professor Kolb's reading makes extensive reference to both history and the texts of popular culture.

"High Noon at Yellow Sky"

Harold H. Kolb, Jr.

I

Let's begin with the classic American Western, and then see how Stephen Crane's "The Bride Comes to Yellow Sky" clarifies and complicates the genre. Crane's tale is a parody of the heroic adventure story of the American West that began with bits and pieces of eighteenth- and nineteenth-century frontier legends and sketches, gathered shape in Cooper's *Leatherstocking Tales*, blossomed profusely with the creation of the dime novel in 1860 and the publication of Bret Harte's mining camp stories in the *Overland Monthly* starting in 1868, and was converted to both indoor and outdoor theatre by Buffalo Bill Cody.[2] The first dime novel—*Malaeska; The Indian Wife of the White Hunter*—was a Western, and it led a procession of thousands of titles and hundreds of thousands of copies down to the end of the nineteenth century, when the narrative conventions of the genre were so firmly in place that Crane could assume, and thus deviate from, a clear set of reader expectations.

No thoughtful reader, of course, would claim historical accuracy for these romantic tales—as much products of the East as of the West—with their stainless-steel heroes, double-dyed villains, imperiled maidens, tall-tale exploits, and cleanly won moral victories. They are countered by our real-life experiences, as well as by the explosion of research about the real American West, inaugurated by Frederick Jackson Turner in 1893, which has taught us that working cowboys didn't wear guns, that the West was won more by families than by steely-eyed masculine isolates, and that Wyatt Earp's duties as a peace officer included subduing drunks (the main duty for Western police), repairing boardwalks, and dragging dead animals off the streets.[3]

---

2. Cody played himself on stage from 1872 to 1882, and founded Buffalo Bill's Wild West show in 1883.

3. Turner's famous 1893 essay, which re-routed the study of American history, claimed that "The existence of an area of free land, its continuous recession, and the advance of American settlement westward, explain American development." See Taylor.

Western towns were no more violent than Eastern cities; one study of the rip-roaring Western cattle towns concludes that the average number of homicides, per town, was 1.5 a year (White 330).

Nevertheless, the stereotypic Western rolled on into the twentieth century, gathering new strength and wider audiences as it was adapted for motion pictures (the first movie, an eight-minute reel entitled "The Great Train Robbery," was a Western) and television (which, in the high-water year of 1959, offered viewers 30 different Western serials). In spite of new media, the codes and conventions established in the nineteenth century were passed on relatively unchanged until the mid-twentieth century. *The Virginian* perfectly demonstrates this process. Originally a hugely popular novel by Owen Wister published in 1902, it was based in part on earlier stories he had issued in the 1890s. A stage version of *The Virginian*, written by Wister and producer Kirk La Shelle and starring Dustin Farnum, opened at the Manhattan Theatre in New York on 5 January 1904, ran for four months, and then went on the road for a decade. The play script became the basis for subsequent film versions in 1914 (an early silent film starring Farnum and directed by Cecil B. de Mille), 1923 (also a silent film), 1929 (with Gary Cooper in the title role), and 1946 (in Technicolor, with Joel McCrea, Brian Donlevy, and Sonny Tufts). The name, though not the story, was reborn in 1962, in an NBC TV series that ran for nine years.

The Western romance became such a fixed form in the second half of the nineteenth century and the first half of the twentieth that we can investigate it anywhere, before Stephen Crane or after, and find precisely the same elements. Thus we can use *High Noon*, a film made in 1952, to represent the stereotypes Crane discovered in nineteenth-century dime novels and theatre performances, and parodied in "The Bride" in 1898. *High Noon* is a good choice to represent the classic Western, since its spare, stripped-down presentation perfectly embodies the clichés of a century of popular fiction, illustrations, and stage, film, and television re-enactments.[4] *High Noon* is pure cliché, brilliantly presented and so distilled that its entire 84-minute action of confrontation, shootout, and resolution occupies only six pages of Wister's 300-page novel.

---

4. And of course, like all art, the film's own moment in history provides new applications for those clichés. The confrontational politics of the early Cold War led many viewers to make both national and international analogies—standing up to Senator McCarthy at home and facing down the Soviets abroad.

The elements of *High Noon* are starkly composed and easily summarized: a cowardly town, a quartet of villains, a beautiful bride, and a heroic town marshal, played by Gary Cooper with the laconic, gee whiz Ma'am, physical and moral competence that characterized his portrayal of the Virginian 23 years earlier, as well as his portrayal of the protagonists in half a dozen other Western films. *High Noon* begins on Sunday morning, at 10:40. Wedding vows are just being exchanged by the marshal, Will Kane, and his Quaker bride (played by Grace Kelly, in her first film). The frontier town, with its dusty streets, frame houses, and unpainted storefronts, dozes in the sun. Then a telegram arrives. The marshal, about to retire from office, learns that an old enemy has just been released from prison. Having sworn revenge against the marshal who brought him to justice, the freed murderer is due in shortly on the noon train. Armed companions await him at the depot.

The townspeople hunt their holes, advising the marshal to flee; his wife pleads for non-violence. The newlyweds start away in a buckboard, but suddenly the marshal turns the horses around. He knows that a man cannot run from his fate. He returns to an empty-appearing town, determined to stay and meet the killers even though his bride deserts him, and the townspeople—some cowardly, some indecisive, some cynical—will not assist him. As the minutes tick away, the marshal loads his Colt .45, straps on his gun belt, and steps into the deserted streets.

Meanwhile Kane's bride, fleeing to the thin safety of the hotel, confronts a voluptuous Mexican señora, Mrs. Ramirez, who seems somewhat too concerned about the marshal's welfare. Apparently, however, he had rejected her, and she tells the bride that they have not spoken for a year. "If Kane were my man," says Señora Ramirez, "I'd never leave him like [you are]. I'd get a gun; I'd fight."

The whistle of the train cuts across the prairie; the hands of the clock move relentlessly toward the zenith.[5] The released killer arrives, receives his six-shooter from his waiting cohorts, and leads the unshaven quartet into the silent town. The arrival is heard behind closed doors, watched from behind drawn shades.

At 12 o'clock we have the walkdown duel in the sun. The marshal encounters the revenge party and a flurry of gunfire explodes the silence. Kane kills two of the bad men and is wounded himself. His

---

5. One wonders if the intense focus on the clock in *High Noon*, whose 84 minutes of playing time duplicate the time of the action, owes a debt to Crane's tale.

Quaker bride, watching from a window, grabs a pistol and shoots the third villain as he stops to reload. The marshal finishes off the leader, and the streets are silent once more. The townspeople, ashamed, gather round as the wounded marshal and his woman climb into their buggy. He throws his tin star to the ground and they ride off toward the distant plains, followed only by the double-edged refrain—"Do not forsake me, oh my darling, on this our wedding day."[6]

There you have the classic Western, with its conventions and stereotypes intact—a fossilized form virtually unchanged for almost a century. At its centre is the sheriff-hero, a six-gun virtuoso who protects the town from outlaws, and from itself. He is lean, tough, honest, and can knock a man out of his saddle with the disdainful grace of a Renaissance courtier.

He never shoots unless he must, but when he does he never misses. He is often an awkward, unpolished outdoors sort of lover, but he always gets the girl; or wins her heart only to break it as he rides alone into the sunset. This knight of the plains, as Wister saw him, is a lawman or a righteous citizen or a reformed renegade forced to take the law into his own hands, usually for one last time. He is often a loner, the last of a dying breed of solitary defenders of justice.

And there is the pure young maiden, dainty but strong, timid but courageous, whose charms are the reward for a straight-shooting marshal, whose white breast is the natural resting place for the dusty, world-weary head of the protector of the people.

And then there is a villainous bad man, or men, often in threes or fours—stubble-bearded, hard-drinking, foul-talking, sharp-shooting

---

6. The persistence of the fixed formulas of the classic Western can be seen in the 1986 film *Top Gun*, which might be called an aerial Western. In addition to the title phrase "Top Gun," which is what Navy pilots call the Fighter Weapons School in Miramar, California, the climaxing duel in the sky follows precisely the odds against the hero and the rhythm of confrontation seen in *High Noon*. Maverick (Tom Cruise) shoots down three of the bad guys (in this case MIG 21s); his partner nails one. The lesson learned also is identical—Do not forsake me, oh my wingman, on this our combat day. And Maverick, of course, gets the girl after, and because of, the battle. What is extraordinary about the classic Western is how long it lasted, and still lasts. What is extraordinary about Crane's tale is how clearly he understood the genre as early as 1898.

(except when firing at the hero), sadistic—chaos come again with its threat of destruction, murder, and rape, the latter implied symbolically in *High Noon*, when Ben Miller, the ex-convict's brother, breaks a plate-glass window with his pistol, pulls a woman's hat from the display case, and hangs it on his belt like a scalp.[7]

It is, presumably, the Old West—cactus and sagebrush, wild and violent, spawning human evil. But it is a wild West finally corralled, tamed by the dead-eye dexterity and bronzed integrity of the most enduring of all American folk heroes—the cowboy-marshal of the perpetually vanishing West. The power of *High Noon* lies in the stark terseness, the clarity with which it presents all the clichés, done to a turn. This is the power that Philip Morris, Inc. discovered when, shortly after *High Noon* was released, they started searching for a "lean, relaxed outdoorsman" to use in a new advertising campaign for Marlboro cigarettes, one of the first filtered cigarette brands and one that initially had been "a premium-priced, ivory-and beauty-red-tipped luxury cigarette made and marketed exclusively for the fastidious female" (O'Brien 146). They tried "Tattooed Man" aviators and naval officers, and then, in 1955, turned to the cowboy. Eight months later the sales of Marlboros had increased 5,000 per cent.

| 97 |

---

7. This is a brilliant use of symbolism, since the sound of breaking glass alerts Marshal Kane to the location of the villains and enables him to position himself for the encounter. Ben Miller, who has had his eye on Kane's pretty bride, is the first man the marshal shoots.

II

Our word parody comes to us, via Latin, from the Greek words *para*, "beside," as in paramedic; and *oide*, "song," as in ode. Thus a parody is a "song sung beside," an imitation, for the purpose of ridicule or amusement or enlightenment, that depends on the reader's knowledge of the style or genre or text under attack. Stephen Crane's "The Bride" requires us to place, in our minds, the new elements he presents against the well-worn expectations associated with the stereotypic Western, such as *High Noon*. Translated to paper, this contrast can be illustrated as follows:

Expectations in the classic Western	Crane's Version
We expect a handsome, confident, and supremely competent sheriff; lean, cool, and tough; well mounted and well armed.	*Instead we get Jack Potter, a nervous unarmed honeymooner, who rides a train instead of a horse.*
We expect a beautiful maiden, voluptuous but, as Mark Twain put it in Roughing It, *"virtuous to the verge of eccentricity"; or perhaps a delicate young school marm from the East, or a courageous frontier widow; at worst a pretty dancehall girl with a tarnished reputation but a heart of gold.*	*We get a droopy ex-cook from San Anton', who is neither young nor pretty.*
We expect the villain to be a vicious, hard-boiled gunslinger.	*We get Scratchy Wilson, whose main crime seems to be that he can't hold his liquor.*
We expect a dramatic duel in the street.	*We get—nothing.*

The structure of the story points to this letdown. Tension is heightened by the chronological countdown ("'We are due in Yellow Sky at 3.42'"; "'It's seventeen minutes past twelve'"; "The California Express ... was due at Yellow Sky in twenty-one minutes") and the emphasis on the train's movement ("The great Pullman was whirling onward"; "The train was approaching [the Rio Grande] at an angle, and the apex was Yellow Sky.... the distance from Yellow Sky grew shorter.... the hour of Yellow Sky was approaching"; "'We're nearly there'"). The two strands of the plot, on the train and in the "Weary Gentleman" saloon, draw closer and closer together until they reach the climax—which is, of course, an anti-climax.

We expect gunplay and violence and death.	*Instead, the only shots fired are at a dog, a door, and some windows. At the conclusion we have the inappropriateness of gunplay, the collapse of violence, and no death.*
We expect a marriage at the end, or the couple riding off into the sunset.	*We get the marriage at the beginning and the end reveals only that the ex-cook is about to begin her kitchen chores once more.*

All the clichés of the Western appear to be overturned.

Yet, and this is a measure of Crane's acuity, "anti-climax" and "parody" do not fully explain the tale. In some ways it is also a straight, a classic Western. Jack Potter is a courageous man; he does defend the entire town. He has faced Scratchy Wilson on a drunken tear before and he faces him down again. Although Potter is unarmed, "his heels had not moved an inch backward." In this last confrontation, Scratchy reacts to the news that the marshal fires at him three times—"'I'm married ... married. I'm married'"—as if he had been shot: "He moved a pace backward, and his arm with the revolver dropped to his side"; and he drags himself away, leaving "funnel-shaped tracks in the heavy sand" (384).

Crane also realizes that the one-last-time aspect of the classic Western, its quality of capturing life in the process of change, does have historical validity even if it is overdone in popular fiction. Most of what we think of as trans-Mississippi Western history—explorations, fur trapping, Overland Trail migrations, farming settlements, mining booms, buffalo hunts, Indian wars, the opening up and then the closing down of the free-range cattle industry—happened at breakneck speed as a populous, ambitious, land-hungry, technological society spilled across a continent and over the neolithic native populations the continent contained. This entire history, from the rendezvous of the mountain men to the stringing of barbed wire that Frederick Remington captures in his 1895 oil painting "The Fall of the Cowboy," could be encompassed within the life span of a single individual. Joe Walker, born six years before Lewis and Clark and their "Corps of Discovery" started up the Missouri in 1804, was a trapper and trader, an explorer of the Great Salt Lake and Yosemite Valley, the leader of a party of emigrants in 1843, a guide for J.C. Frémont, a miner, and a cattle dealer. He served for a time as sheriff of Jackson County, Missouri.

| 100 |

The fictional Scratchy Wilson, "about the last one of the old gang that used to hang out along the river" (382), and Marshal Potter have become displaced persons, for the American West kept vanishing, changing, being transformed.[8] Crane manages to get both history and burlesque into his tale. The plains of Texas are "pouring eastward" (377); Scratchy wears a shirt "made on the east side of New York" and boots "of the kind beloved in winter by little sledding boys on the hillsides of New England" (382); the horse—none are mentioned in Yellow Sky—is now the iron horse; the cowboy has been replaced by a porter. The bride—curtains, churches, civilization—has come to Yellow Sky just as Oliver Ward's bride came to the mining town of Leadville in Wallace Stegner's *Angle of Repose*, where she is introduced as "our civilizing influence"; just as the schoolmarm, the Virginian's bride-to-be, comes to Bear Creek, Wyoming:

> The schoolhouse ... symbolized the dawn of a neighborhood, and it brought a change into the wilderness air. The feel of it struck cold upon the free spirits of the cow-punchers, and they told each other that, what with women and children and wire fences, this country would not long be a country for men. (63)

In "The Bride Comes to Yellow Sky," Stephen Crane has taken the clichés of the American Western and made fun of them, while seeing, behind these clichés, whatever historical insights the classic Western offered as well as its timeless appeal of heroic action in a world full of danger. The climax is an anti-climax, but the anti-climax is also a climax. Crane had honed this sense of multiplicity in the novel he wrote just before heading west in 1893, in which war is both heroic

---

8. But they appear in one more Crane story, "Moonlight on the Snow," published in 1900, in which Jack Potter, "a famous town marshal of Yellow Sky," is now sheriff of the entire county, with Scratchy Wilson as his deputy. Vol. V of the Virginia edition: *Tales of Adventure*, 1970, pp. 179-91.

and meaningless, and the novel's last sentence—"Over the river a golden ray of sun came through the hosts of leaden rain clouds"— like the shootout at Yellow Sky, is both climactic and anti-climactic. "The Bride Comes to Yellow Sky" is therefore a logical successor to *The Red Badge of Courage*. Crane's complex vision and his narrative skill in dramatizing complexity, remarkable for any writer but doubly remarkable for one in his mid-twenties, gives us a view of the West that is more acute and more probing than that of most writers who either preceded or followed him.

His tale also demonstrates how appropriate Crane's style could be for comedy, since a joke is always playing at the edge of irony, and humour is forever pointing at tough truths. Our appreciation of "The Bride Comes to Yellow Sky," with its sharp illumination of the American West and its redemption of the notoriously superficial genre of parody, is deepened by the fact that it is the only comic writing among his major works that Crane—dead of tuberculosis two years after the tale's publication—has left us.[9]

Works Cited

Crane, Stephen. "The Bride Comes to Yellow Sky." *McClure's Magazine* 10 (February 1898): 377–84. Print.

High Noon. Dir. Fred Zimmerman. Prod. Stanley Kramer. 1952. Film.

O'Brien, Robert. "The Executive [i.e., Joseph Cullman], as a Showman." *Esquire* 53 (June 1960): 146–48. Print.

---

9. Crane's story, written two years after his trip to the West and Mexico (January to May 1895) at the age of 23, was published simultaneously in *McClure's Magazine* (U.S.) and *Chapman's Magazine* (England) in February 1898. The most carefully edited modern reprinting is that contained in *Tales of Adventure*, ed. Fredson Bowers, with an intro. by J.C. Levenson. Vol. V of the *Works of Stephen Crane* (Charlottesville: University Press of Virginia, 1970). See 109–20 for the text of "The Bride Comes to Yellow Sky," which "attempts to reconstruct as nearly as the preserved documents permit the typescript used as copy by *McClure's Magazine*, with the addition of the Heinemann final alteration." See also Introduction, xxvii-xl, lxxiii-lxxvii; Textual Introduction, clxxii-clxxvi; Textual Notes, 205–6; Editorial Emendations in the Copy-Text, 219–20. Crane wrote 30 other Western works, most of them based on his 1895 trip, which are collected in various combinations in volumes V and VIII of the Virginia edition, and in Frank Bergon, ed., *The Western Writings of Stephen Crane* (New York: New American Library, 1979).

Taylor, George Rogers, ed. *The Turner Thesis Concerning the Role of the Frontier in American History.* 3rd ed. Lexington, MA: D.C. Heath, 1972. Print.

White, Richard. *"It's Your Misfortune and None of My Own": A History of the American West.* Norman: U of Oklahoma P, 1991. Print.

Wister, Owen. *The Virginian: A Horseman of the Plains.* New York: Macmillan, 1902; rep. Boston: Houghton Mifflin, 1968. Print.

Some Points to Consider

- Review the interview with Harold Kolb, Jr. What does he say about the approaches he uses in his essay? How does he use his knowledge of history and popular culture to shed light on "The Bride"?

- How does he blend his cultural and formalist approaches?

- Do you find the comparison between the film *High Noon* and the short story "The Bride" illuminating? Why did Kolb choose to focus on this film? Would choosing another Western film have worked as well?

- What is the purpose and effect of all the information on the American Western genre (presented in the opening paragraphs)?

- The author rehearses a great deal of background information before ever discussing "The Bride" in detail. Do you find this strategy effective?

- Compare Kolb's opening discussion of genre and stereotypes with Clifford Geertz's discussion of "winking." How does the strategy of "thick description" work to enhance our appreciation of the issues raised?

- Does Kolb help you appreciate the complexity of the issues raised?

- Kolb speaks as an authority on American literature. What makes his essay authoritative? Are there ways that a student critic might take a similar stance?

Exercises

Field Stance

The following final set of questions asks you to enter the conversation initiated by two of the foregoing authors. Here you are asked to "take issue" with the authors.

1. In her essay on "The Bride," Katherine Sutherland makes passing reference to what she calls a "vaguely anti-Semitic" characterization—an observation that she leaves undeveloped. At one level, Crane's reference to Jewish women and Scratchy's shirt simply underscores the East-West theme of the story. However, the reference taps into a network of associations very common a century ago, but no longer alive to most readers today. The American garment industry, especially the less expensive and less fashionable end of that industry, was for generations concentrated in the lower east side of Manhattan. As in much of Europe, a high percentage of the workers in the garment industry were Jewish. The historical circumstances that had resulted in this concentration go something like this: over many centuries of European history, Jews were subject to severe restrictions on the types of jobs they could hold. Tailoring was a trade usually open to Jews, and though it was not particularly lucrative, it was considered a relatively attractive option in that one's skill was readily transportable if the level of persecution in a particular area suddenly increased. Out of this background a tradition grew up in America, as well, of Jewish garment manufacturers (usually male) and of more impoverished lower-end female garment workers (also largely Jewish). Given this context, what associations with the adjective "Jewish" may Crane have tapped into or reinforced with his description? Is Sutherland's characterization of the reference to Jewish women as "vaguely anti-Semitic" justified?

In your response journal, take Sutherland's passing reference and, using the notes above as a starting point, discuss how you might develop it into an essay topic.

2. Alice Farley's concise essay on "The Bride" may seem, at first glance, detached and analytical. Yet, as her personal narrative (see Chapter 6) on the writing of the essay attests, Farley's process is anything but detached. She is methodical in her research, but also open to chance inspiration. Farley's narrative gives us an especially detailed peek behind the scenes at a critic in action.

Consider how Farley's critical process matches up with Kolb's three-stage process for developing a critical issue. Also consider how (and why) Farley adapts her personal reading (and teaching) of Crane's story to the more formal demands of publishing an article in *The Explicator*. One demand that a journal like *The Explicator* makes on its authors is the need to say a lot about a little: the journal publishes only short papers, about the size of a short undergraduate essay. It is understandable, therefore, that one or two points might remain tantalizingly undeveloped in an article like Farley's. Her concluding paragraph, for instance, makes reference to Crane's poetic sensibility, suggesting that he was "peculiarly sensitive" to issues of word choice. Many of the names cited, though, have strong religious connotations, and one might be justified in wondering whether Crane's interest in the rituals of Christian funerals and names like "Old Scratch" might have as much to do with his religious upbringing (his father was a Baptist minister) as with his calling as a poet.

Find out as much as you can about Crane's religious background and, using the notes above as a starting point, take issue with Farley's claim that his choice of words is linked only to a poet's sensitivity for language. In your response journal, write several paragraphs exploring the relationship between Crane's religious upbringing and his use of religious names, images, and rituals.

(You might also want to consider a recent critical essay that you have written and, following Farley's model in Chapter 6, describe your own critical process—provide a retrospective description of how you actually wrote the essay. What "field constraints" and/or assumptions affected the way you translated your initial reader response into a formal essay?)

CHAPTER 5

Reading and Writing about Poetry

Overview

In this chapter you'll be introduced to important ways of thinking and writing about poetry. We'll begin by exploring some definitions, noting poetry's origins in song and ritual. Next, you'll read Robert Kroetsch's "This Part of the Country," a contemporary poem about reading, writing, seeing, and exploring. The poem echoes some of the Western patterns you encountered when reading Crane's short story: an emphasis on landscape and place, on feeling "out of place," on images of time and colour and movement. You will likely find the experience of reading the poem quite different from reading the short story, however. To enhance your appreciation of the poem, and to help you read and write about poetry generally, I've included an interview with the author. Next, you'll be given a critical tool kit, including a review of the special technical language and considerations critics typically attend to when writing essays on poetry. We'll employ this tool kit to write, step-by-step, a sample essay on Kroetsch's poem. The chapter concludes with the complete texts of those classic poems quoted as examples.

"Poetry!" said Scratchy, not at all comprehending.

Some Opening Thoughts about Poetry

"Poetry isn't written from the idea down. It's written from the phrase, line and stanza up, which is different from what your teacher taught you to do in school."

Margaret Atwood

"Poetry ... should strike the reader as a wording of his own highest thoughts, and appear almost a remembrance."

John Keats

"Poetry is like making a joke. If you get one word wrong at the end of a joke, you have lost the whole thing."

W.S. Merwin

"The joy of poetry is that it will wait for you. Novels don't wait for you. Characters change. But poetry will wait."

Sonia Sanchez

"[Poetry is] hundreds of things coming together at the right moment."

Elizabeth Bishop

"Poetry is what gets lost in translation."

Robert Frost

"Poetry Should Not Mean / But Be"

It's natural for writers, especially poets, to reflect on their art—on the creative process, including a coming to terms with poetic inspiration, poetic form, and the effect of poetry on its audience. We can learn a lot by listening to writers: "A poem," says Archibald Macleish, "should not mean / But be." Poetry's roots are in song, in the ritual chanting, rhythmic clapping, stamping, and dancing of ancient peoples expressing themselves communally. Beginning with laments, ritual celebrations, and elementary hymns—and later lullabies, elegies, work songs, and play songs—poetry originated in oral expression, in performance.

These rhythms are all around us, in the cycle of day and night, in the tides and the seasons; they are inside us, in the movement of our blood, as inspiration and exhalation, the beat of a pulse. Poetry gives formal expression to these rhythms. It is, at root, not only about "meaning," but about "being." Poetry records and creates personal and communal experiences. Poetry is also about language, for language too has its rhythms and patterns. Language is musical.

Reading a Poem

Reading and writing about poetry takes time. But, as American poet Sonia Sanchez reminds us, "poetry ... will wait for you." Let's begin by first experiencing a sample poem, and then consider the meaning.

First, the poem. Please read it aloud. Ask others to read it aloud | 107 | and listen to the reading as a form of vocal interpretation.

Once you've truly heard the poem, then begin to ask questions of the text. Read it again (this time in silence) with pen or pencil in hand. In the margin, jot down your thoughts, noting those places where your expectations are challenged. At first, you might look for key words that stand out because of their sound quality, their unusual word choice, their position in the line (words placed at the end of each line tend to carry more emphasis), and so on. Look also for key images, especially those that suggest contradiction, paradox, or otherwise surprise you. Listen to the rhythms and sounds, and whether these complement or contradict the sense of the poem. Consider the organization of each part and the relationship of one part to the others. Is the organization associative? Is it logical? Note any words or references that might be unfamiliar.

Once you've made some preliminary notes, try to identify as many patterns and issues as possible, and discuss the poem with others in your class. Compare notes and form your own response to the poem *before* proceeding to the interview with the poet.

"This Part of the Country"

i. Kamloops: Late Arrival

Searching for the mountain,
we found a shoe.

After the first drought
we dreamed a river.
After the forecast city
we listened for rain.

The fallen roof and fireweed
conspire.
    Seeds too explode.

Iamb and jackhammer in duet:
silence, breaking the drum:
the city, climbing, climbing.

Two rivers, then, coming together.

2. This Part of the Country

In this part of the country, the horizon is a glacier.
One morning the horses of the sun lost all direction.

David Thompson, that very afternoon, found west. He saw
a man on a sandbar, sluicing for pieces of light.

I saw George Bowering riding a yellow horse, that high country
    poet
wearing no gun. His horse had eyes the color of bullets.

In this part of the country, sagebrush is a version of dance.
    You must
enter in slowly. This is where train robbers learn their moves.

I saw Roy Miki wading in Sheila Watson's river. He was fishing
with a line made of blue memory. The sky was tinder dry.

3. Blue River: Checking In

Somewhere west and south of Mt Robson
I forgot my name. This much I remember.
It was a long, white drive; I was alone.
The patient trees were shrouded in snow.

The woman behind the motel desk
said I would have to sign my name.
Snow had fallen, I explained, and it fell;
the road was not to be found.
We were both surprised by the dark.

Some days night is a voluntary silence.
Then one of us asked (was it she
or I?), So how did you get here?

4. This Part of the Country

Landscape is a diagram of the impossible. Why do we have to
look at a tree to see the wind? How do we tell the frozen lake
from future interrogations?

Today in Kamloops the snowline slid slowly all day long down
into the valley of the North Thompson River. First my head
turned a hummocky white. Then my shoulders became slopes
for elegant white toboggans. Then all my fingers assumed the
dignity of ice. It was a slow procedure. When I went to move
my feet I couldn't find them.

Here in this part of the country the so-called visibility, from
airplanes and avalanches alike, is the equivalent of zero. We
measure our descent by exhalation, hoping to see each breath
freeze as it escapes the mouth. Is that a question or an answer?

Entering into the Poem

Like the speaker trying to find his place in a new community, I'd
encourage you to "enter in slowly." Resist, at first, the temptation
of narrative and the natural habit of trying to pin down the text's
meaning. Ask instead, "How does the poem affect me?" The advice
that follows refocuses attention on the kind of formal attributes often
considered in passing during a first reading:

Read for sound: Listen to the music of the words and try to catch the
rhythm and pace of the lines. The sounds contain a kind of *embodied
meaning*, a reminder of past experiences. Canadian poet Margaret
Atwood tells us that she doesn't "think of poetry as a 'rational' activity but as an aural one." In an interview with Joyce Carol Oates she
elaborates:

> My poems usually begin with words or phrases which appeal
> more because of their sound than their meaning, and the move-
> ment and phrasing of a poem are very important to me. But

like many modern poets I tend to conceal rhymes by placing them in the middle of lines, and to avoid immediate alliteration and assonance in favour of echoes placed later in the poems. For me, every poem has a texture of sound which is at least as important to me as the "argument." This is not to minimize "statement." But it does annoy me when students, prompted by the approach of their teacher, ask, "What is the poet trying to say?" It implies that the poet is some sort of verbal cripple who can't quite "say" what he "means" and has to resort to a lot of round-the-mulberry-bush, thereby putting the student to a great deal of trouble extracting his "meaning," like a prize out of a box of Cracker Jacks. ("Margaret Atwood: Poet," *The New York Times* 21 May 1978)

Ask yourself what mood or meaning the sounds convey. Why are the sounds (the open "o"s, the hissing "s"s, the explosive "p"s, and so on) effective? Does the rhythm contribute to this mood? The rhymes? How? What do the sounds tell you about the speaker's attitude?

Read for emotion and stance: You might consider, for example, what feelings and sense perceptions are conveyed at various points in the poem. Do you share them? Have you experienced similar sensations? The poem's mood: Does it change? Where? And how does the change in mood affect your reading? The poem's imagery: What emotional responses or personal associations do the images provoke? What images stand out for you? Can you say why? Can you describe the pattern or design the images make? The references to shoes and walking, for example? How would you describe the speaker's relationship to the landscape? His perspective or stance? How does it change?

Read for structure: How is the poem organized? Is there a logical or emotional progression of parts (e.g., stanzas or verse paragraphs)? A shift in mood or tone at certain points in the poem? Does the speaker's attitude, stance, or understanding shift at key points? If so, why? In other words, how does the poem's structure contribute to our experience of reading the poem? When responding to structure, try not to read line-by-line, in a linear manner; as Robert Kroetsch advises in the following interview, "the reader can dodge around, and should, in order to engage rather than just receive."

Read for language: Can you identify key words or phrases? What makes them stand out? What is the relationship between these words and the mood created? Why have some details been included and others left out? At which points in the poem do you experience surprise? Do the words and phrases and images contribute to that surprise? How? Consider what Kroetsch says about the *focusing line* of his poem (in the interview below)—about how an overheard phrase inspired the poem.

Read for theme: Once you've answered these questions you can begin to read for theme: What is the poem saying to you? Ask yourself, in general terms, what aspects of human experience is the poem addressing? Why has the poet focused on these aspects? How does the poet communicate his experience? Remember that the poem's *why* and *how* are as important as (or arguably more important than) the *what*: accounting for the poem's meaning is more than a matter of offering a simple paraphrase. As Kroetsch explains, even for the poet, meaning is difficult to capture:

> Consider the simple and impossible task of describing a landscape. Or love of place. It's not just a matter of using metaphor. No, not that at all. Rather, we present images in a poem, and the images let the poet say, This is not quite what I'm trying to say, but it's as close as I can get at the moment. So here's another image. And here's another.

In the following interview, Robert Kroetsch provides a poet's perspective on *writing*, *reading*, and *writing about* his poetry.

An Interview with a Poet

Robert Kroetsch is one of Canada's leading poets and critics, someone recognized internationally for both his writing and teaching. Born in Heisler, Alberta, he attended the University of Alberta and, later, the University of Iowa. A Governor General's Literary Award winner and appointed an Officer of the Order of Canada in 2004, he has written over 25 works of fiction, poetry, and criticism, including, with William Spanos, *Boundary 2*, a journal of postmodern literary theory. Kroetsch turned to writing poetry in the 1970s, eventually authoring 14 collections. His major books of poetry include *The Stone Hammer Poems* (1975), *Seed Catalogue* (1977), *The Sad Phoenician* (1979), *Field Notes* (1981), *Advice to My Friends* (1985), *Excerpts from the Real World* (1986), *Completed Field Notes* (1989), *The Hornbooks of Rita K* (2001), and *The Snowbird Poems* (2004). His autobiography, *A Likely Story: The Writing Life*, was published in 1995. Kroetsch died in a car accident in 2011.

It is unusual for poets to write or speak directly about their own work. Margaret Atwood's attitude, as posted on her official website, is typical:

> Often students and curious readers write to ask questions about an interpretation of one of my books, questions such as, "This book ends ambiguously. We aren't really told what happened to Character X. Can you tell me what really happened?" … or sometimes, "Critic X says Y about your use of Z. Do you agree?" There are two points to be made about this sort of question. First, what I think about what happened is already in the book. Secondly, I'm not comfortable giving interpretations of my work. If I were to provide one, it would become the definitive interpretation, inhibiting readers from finding their own meanings. <http://www.margaretatwood.ca/faq.php>

Sometimes, however, poets offer more direct information about their writing processes, usually via interviews or during public readings of their work. Robert Kroetsch's interview, for example, provides us with an extraordinary view of the care, craft, creativity, and sense of audience it takes to write a poem.

Kroetsch has been called the great "mythologizer of the Canadian West," someone who listens carefully to the vernacular, to everyday voices.

Would you talk about the writing of "This Part of the Country"? How did the poem develop?

"This Part of the Country" is ambiguously a travel poem and an arrival poem. It began—it came to mind, as we say—quite literally in the space between travel and arrival. I was driving the Yellowhead from Winnipeg to Kamloops, where I was to work with other writers as a visiting writer-in-residence. Caught in a heavy mountain snowstorm, I stopped overnight in Valemount. I had hoped to get as far as Blue River. Even then, I was located and dislocated.

Next day at noon I stopped for coffee and a bite to eat in the town of Barriere, pausing to gather my thoughts before driving into Kamloops. While sipping coffee I listened in on the conversation taking place at the table next to mine. An older man was telling his companion about the logging in the area. "In this part of the country," he told her, not once but three times, "we ...." And he went on to explain how they used to log in the North Thompson valley.

I was driving away when I realized the speaker had given me the theme of something I should write. And I had not really planned to write anything; I was wilfully leaving myself open to surprise, and that surprise might well be silence itself.

In "this part of the country." That phrase gave me a focus, place, a track into memory, the possibility of arrival. It gave me words and a story. At last, I was able to drive into the city.

Did you choose a specific poetic form for "This Part of the Country"?

I have long admired that Japanese poet, Basho, who in the seventeenth century travelled through northern Japan, at once writing a prose account of his journey and the short, lyric poems he was compelled into writing. Kamloops too is a place, "a western landscape" where prose and poetry speak to each other, give each other sustenance and inspiration, at once collide and invigorate. The forked rivers become a place of fusion and opening. The differing voices give weight to each other's concerns.

This is where the individual and community collaborate. The silence speaks; the speaking allows both travel and arrival, becoming and being. The poem escapes the poet, becomes vital memory.

I notice that the line length changes dramatically, becoming very long by the end of the poem. Is this related to Basho's practice as well?

Writing about Literature: A Guide for the Student Critic

My poem becomes more inclusive as the lines get longer. As Basho so well demonstrates, the poem is often looking for a balance between the wish to include everything and yet the need to give the poem a certain and telling shape of its own, a precision of emotion and idea and detail.

Is "This Part of the Country" influenced by the work of other poets?

Poets talk to each other. Poems talk to each other. One of our pleasures as readers is the act of overhearing. In this poem I talk to and with the writers I name. Sheila Watson is a marvel of vision and exactness. Roy Miki dares to investigate ideas of home and homelessness, search and surrender. George Bowering likes the borderlands of each word, inviting us to hear the word itself as a site of inclusiveness and shape. Place is at the centre of my poem, but place is always shifting, reaching, at once being changed by the poet and changing the poet. That power of transformation is part of the appeal of poetry. It is one of our reasons for entering into the delightful and dangerous activity called reading.

As a teacher, how do you encourage your students to enter into a meaningful dialogue with poetry? And, even more specifically, how would you like to see "This Part of the Country" taught?

I often ask students to read a passage aloud in class. I encourage them to feel the physical presence, and the physical pleasure, of the poem. On the tongue. In one's ears. Poetry is language and sound and memory and surprise. Feel the rub of the poem, what one might call the surface of the poem, before worrying about depths. Experience what one might call the erotics of the poem. Allow the poem its potential. But also allow your own potential to find itself in the poem. I suppose I'd like a reader of my poem to try reading it aloud, even if the speech is only in one's mind. Discover the rhythms of the poem, any poem, the images and ideas and words and patterns that make the poem a poem.

I suspect that becoming attuned to poetry takes both time and practice. Can you say more about how rhythm works—perhaps noting a place where rhythm, image, word, and pattern work to make "This Part of the Country" a poem?

Will, I wouldn't try to tell a student how to read my poem, but I will share a concern I had in the making of the poem. At the poem's end I had to get back to the opening in some way and when, in the second-to-last stanza, I wrote the sentence, "When I went to move my feet I couldn't find them," I had a good feeling. I was echoing the opening stanza. Feet and standing still and walking, and walking itself a special rhythm that connects with the earth, with place. The verb "find" going back to all the poem's concern with the act of "looking for" and the recurring word "found." Having myself found the image of the snow-buried or disappeared feet, I could move into the final stanza, and the conclusion that echoes the contraries that sometimes shape the poem. I could move to the overview that leads to an understanding of zero and the process of seeing. I could move to the last words that ask, "Is that a question or an answer?" You see? You've got to dodge around, not follow the track suggested by the "and then and then" of the words on the page.

Is this true for the way readers compose meaning as well? Following the track suggested by the words on the page— that is, reading the poem line-by-line, in sequence, and neglecting to also "dodge around"—may produce an incomplete interpretation?

Yes, one of the special things about reading is the way we can speed up or slow down, reread, or stop reading for a bit and reflect. The reader can dodge around, and should, in order to engage rather than just receive. The reader, as you say, composes meaning. That is, we have much inherited or shared meaning in our culture and in ourselves, but we also want to make meaning as we read—we want to make sense (what a wonderful expression) of our own experiences, our own lives. The magic resides in our ability to look at those marks on the page, those words and sentences in print, and make of them stories, histories, autobiographies, jokes and tragedies, messages and emotions and even other people.

Your poem seems to describe a similar experience. That when we "read" the landscape—or, in the case of your poem's speaker, when he reads himself into the landscape—we find that meaning is never completely fixed or static. "Landscape is a diagram of the impossible." The poem's imagery invokes a pattern of deferral and indirection—of experiencing something in terms of something else. Does good poetry invite such complex reader response—more so than, say, prose fiction?

Yes, I like your saying that in poetry we experience "something in terms of something else." That is, the poem tries to name the unnamable, speak the unspeakable. Consider the simple and impossible task of describing a landscape. Or love of place. It's not just a matter of using metaphor. No, not that at all. Rather, we present images in a poem, and the images let the poet say, This is not quite what I'm trying to say, but it's as close as I can get at the moment. So here's another image. And here's another. Again as you say, deferral and indirection. That's as close as we can get, and getting close is exciting stuff. This movement through thoughts and images becomes the method of my poem, and I suppose I'm saying that poetry is always trying to make things simple but at the same time getting itself entangled in the difficult. Prose fiction is written in some strange way to be read faster. A poem is always slowing us down. Maybe the stanza form does some of that slowing down. Or maybe rhyme and stress do that too. I'm just wondering now; I can't say I know. The great fiction writers, like Crane, are trying to get at the unnamable, but they use different strategies. The notion of a scene is different in prose fiction than it is in poetry—different versions of economy. Both stay fluid. Prose fiction and poetry, when they're hitting on all cylinders, elude a final meaning. Thus we are kept ever busy as readers.

Wasn't it Coleridge who said that "prose equals words in their best order; poetry equals the best words in the best order"? As you say, "different versions of economy." By way of conclusion, would you offer some final words of advice to students writing about poetry? How do students move from critical reading to effective critical writing?

It seems to me that the key lies in reading lots of poetry. Read in the tradition, British and American and Canadian. Read your contemporaries to find out what is happening now. New poetry is news about our lives. Choose a couple of your favourite poets and read lots of their work, to get a sense of how individual poems become parts of larger shapes. The immersion in poetry will lead you to musing about patterns, intentions, strategies, images, symbols, told and assumed stories, mythic and emotional structures, poetic voices. Poems have voices. Reading poems compels us into talking. We learn to talk with friends and fellow students about poetry; we learn to talk to and with poems about poetry. Reading compels us into writing. Good critical writing is sensual as well as intellectual; it engages the senses as well as the mind. Accept the pleasures that poetry offers—the pleasures of being in the world, not outside it. Write from that ground. Give yourself permission to respond abundantly. Careful reading will lead you to discover your own marvelous ability to write.

Exercises

Social Stance and Institutional Stance

1. Discuss the interview with others in the class. Did the interview resolve any questions you had about the poem? Did it create new questions?

2. Interview (if possible) other creative writers on campus—say, someone teaching and someone studying creative writing. Ask them if they agree with Kroetsch's views on reading and writing.

3. Read more poetry by Kroetsch, Basho, Bowering, Watson, and the other authors Kroetsch mentions. Consider what Kroetsch means when he says, "Poets talk to each other. Poems talk to each other."

ACTOR

ACTION

SCENE

BURKE'S
PENTAD

PURPOSE

AGENCY/MEANS

Field Stance

1. Critic and rhetorician Kenneth Burke developed a critical technique called "dramatism," which focuses critical attention on the importance of *motive*: the need or desire that causes a person to act. Significantly, in music, "motive" also refers to a recurrent figure or phrase that develops or gains meaning throughout the composition— and it is in this sense that we can use dramatism to write about poetry. Burke maintains that all of life is dramatic, and that as critics we may discover the motives of others (actors) by identifying their specific motivation as represented in their actions and words. To identify the motive, he proposes that we employ a "Pentad," five questions we can ask of any text. Like the questions asked by a news reporter—Who?

What? When? Where? Why? and How?—the Pentad provides us with a rigorous means of questioning or interviewing a poem:

Action: What happened? What is the nature of the action or act? What is going on?

Scene: Where does the act occur? What is the context? What is the mood or atmosphere? How is the scene represented literally and figuratively?

Actor: Who is involved in the action? What roles are being played? How would you characterize the actor or agent?

Agency/Means: How does the actor or agent act? By what means does he or she act? How are the actions performed?

Purpose: Why does the actor act? What does he or she want? What are the actor's intentions?

Burke encourages you to consider the answers to these questions *in relation* to each other: the relationships, he says, will suggest tensions or potential starting points for developing your analysis of the poem. The most interesting answers will often involve a comparison between, say, scene and actor, or purpose and act. For example, you might take your cue from Kroetsch's interview, where he discusses the act of finding. Ask what he is looking for, and whether what he is looking for changes during the course of the poem. Ask where things are found, literally and figuratively. Ask why the word "found" becomes so important for both the speaker and the author. Ask how the speaker goes about finding his way. Interviewing the poem in this manner should give ample material for a first draft.

2. Try to use the *topoi* (introduced in Chapter 3) to generate an essay on Kroetsch's poem. Take one engaging or surprising or disturbing moment (a key word, phrase, or line; a metaphor or image; a shift in tone or voice or perspective) and consider it in terms of the six *topoi*. Make six headings in your response journal, one for each *topos*, and then jot down how the poetic moment relates to the poem's theme (*contemptus mundi* and complexity); to patterns of duality in the poem (appearance/reality); to other similar images, scenes, actions, rhythms, metaphors, attitudes (everywhereness); to a similar pattern in the real world (paradigm); and to any pattern of contradiction (paradox). Read over your notes and use them to write a sample opening paragraph on Kroetsch's "This Part of the Country."

3. Now reread the Kroetsch interview, looking for ways to supplement or extend your paragraph with direct quotations. Can you identify where the poet addresses each *topos* in his interview?

4. Reconsider question #3 (in the Social Stance and Institutional Stance grouping), this time looking at secondary sources on the authors Kroetsch mentions in his poem. You'll find that the speaker of Kroetsch's poem shares many affinities with the other poets cited. Consider, for example, the significance of the following entry from The Sheila Watson Archives, John M. Kelly Library, University of St. Michael's College, University of Toronto. The archive was recently digitized and made available online:
http://archive.org/details/sheilawatsonarchooston.

Dog Creek, Cariboo Region,
British Columbia

In later reflections of her teaching in the Cariboo, Sheila wrote that "I didn't go there to write about this part of the country. I went there to teach, and that's where I happened to be. I didn't choose it, it chose me. It was the only place in 1934 that said, 'Come, and teach our children.' I had no idea where it was when I left by train in Vancouver, except somewhere there!" Sheila taught in the community, in a single-room school house from 1934 to the fall of 1935. In later reflections, Sheila claimed that she did not produce any relevant writing when she lived in Dog Creek, although she took and preserved a collection of photographs of her life there. "I'd been away for a long time before I realized that if I had something I wanted to say, it was going to be said in these images." It was not until she was walking to work in post-war Toronto that the voices and images of the Cariboo would begin to reveal themselves.

5. Access online Kroetsch's reading of "This Part of the Country." Consider how hearing and seeing the author read and talk about his own work affects your understanding—and perhaps enjoyment—of the poem. Does the reading change your view of the speaker (the agent)? The act, scene, agency, and purpose? Compare the author's comments about the composition of his poem with those presented in the interview: Can you identify how the author's "motive" changes? The online reading: <http://www.smallcities.ca/current_cura/kroetsch.html>

A Critical Tool Kit for Writing about Poetry

Caedmon's Hymn

We begin with an early "song," the Hymn of Creation, the earliest surviving poem in the English language (written between 657 and 680). Like Kroetsch's poem, it both describes and enacts a story of creation and creativity. According to the ancient historian Bede, Caedmon was an illiterate cowherd who knew no poems and was unable to sing. He worked as a labourer at the monastery of Whitby, founded in 657 by St. Hilda. It was common for the workers to gather in a great hall and, for entertainment, pass the harp from hand to hand, inviting each in attendance to sing a poem. Caedmon, knowing nothing of poetry, leaves the hall in shame, as he had often done, and retreats into the nearby stable. As he sleeps, there stands by him in vision one who calls Caedmon by name and asks him to sing. Even in his dreams, Caedmon is forced to face the humiliation of being unable to sing. Bede describes what happens next:

> "Caedmon, sing me something." Then he answered and said: "I do not know how to sing and for that reason I went out from this feast and went hither, because I did not know how to sing at all." Again he said, he who was speaking with him: "Nevertheless, you must sing." Then he said: "What must I sing?" Said he: "Sing to me of the first Creation." When he received this answer, then he began immediately to sing in praise of God the Creator verses and words which he had never before heard. Then he arose from that sleep, and all of those songs which he sang while sleeping he had fast in his memory, and he soon added in the same manner to those words many words of songs worthy of God.

Read aloud the poem that Caedmon reportedly remembers: What mood is created by the sounds alone? By the rhythm?

Caedmon's Hymn: West Saxon Version

> Nu sculon herigean   heofonrices weard,
> meotodes meahte   and his modgeþanc,
> weorc wuldorfæder,   swa he wundra gehwæs,
> ece drihten,   or onstealde.

He ærest sceop   eorðan bearnum
heofon to hrofe,   halig scyppend;
þa middangeard   moncynnes weard,
ece drihten,   æfter teode
firum foldan,   frea ælmihtig.

Literal Translation:

Now we must praise   heaven-kingdom's Guardian,
the Measurer's might   and his mind-plans,
the work of the Glory-Father   when he of wonders of every one,
eternal lord,   the beginning established.

He first created   for the sons of the earth
heaven as a roof,   holy Maker;
then middle-earth   mankind's Guardian;
eternal Lord,   afterwards made
for men the solid ground,   Lord almighty.

One of the intriguing aspects of "Caedmon's Hymn" is that the text comes to us indirectly, in what might be thought of as a secondary source—writing that is one or two steps removed from the original work of literature. Secondary sources provide contexts for critical reading and writing. A secondary source is usually a commentary, a description, an analysis, a discussion, an interview (like the one with Robert Kroetsch), personal letters, or a biographical or autobiographical essay. Caedmon's Hymn is represented (quoted) in Bede's history, but it exists nowhere else. Caedmon's poem exists only as a citation.

University professor Tina Blue offers us some detailed discussion regarding the music of Caedmon's poem. She also suggests how knowing about ancient verse forms can help us appreciate more modern poetry. Blue's field notes provide a secondary source for you to draw upon.

Box 5.1: Field Notes from a Literary Critic

Anglo-Saxon Accentual Meter

Tina Blue

Some Key Terms

alliteration: the repetition of sounds in nearby words; usually the term is used to refer to "initial alliteration," the repetition of sounds at the beginnings of words or syllables, but it can also refer to "internal alliteration," also called "hidden alliteration," where the repeated sounds occur within words or syllables. Sometimes "alliteration" is used to refer to either vowel or consonant sounds, but sometimes it is reserved for repeated consonant sounds.

assonance: a form of alliteration, in which the repeated sounds are vowel sounds rather than consonants.

stressed syllable: a syllable that receives a strong accent.

slack syllable: an unaccented syllable.

caesura (cesura): from the Latin for "cut,"—a strong break or pause in a line of poetry.

distich: a half-line. In Anglo-Saxon poetry, each line is broken into distichs by a heavy caesura.

accentual meter (strong-stress meter; alliterative-stress meter): the metrical pattern used in Anglo-Saxon (Old English) poetry.

accentual-syllabic meter: The metrical pattern found in most English poetry. Accentual-syllabic meter counts both the number of accents and the number of syllables in a line of poetry, whereas accentual meter counts only the number of strong stresses in a line.

meter: from the Greek for "measure." It describes the regular pattern of accented and unaccented syllables in poetry.

scop: the Anglo-Saxon bard. The word comes from the root for "shape" or "make," just as the word "poet" comes from the Greek root for "make."

The oldest metrical system in English poetry, the one used in Anglo-Saxon poetry, is accentual meter (also called strong-stress or alliterative-stress meter). The rhythmic structure of the Anglo-Saxon line is organized by stress and alliteration. Each line is divided into two parts (distichs) by a strong caesura (or pause), with two heavy stresses in each half-line. One or (more usually) both of the stressed syllables in the first distich will alliterate with the first stressed syllable in the second distich. Although the number of stresses in each line is fixed, the number of slack syllables per line is variable.

Two lines of "Caedmon's Hymn" illustrate the metrical structure of Anglo-Saxon poetry:

> He aerest sceop   eorðan bearnum
> Heofon to hrofe   Halig Scyppend

> [**HE AER**est sceop || **Eor**ðan **BE**arnum]
> (He first made || for the sons of the earth

> [**HEO**fon to **HRO**fe || **HAL**ig **SCYP**pend]
> (Heaven as a roof || Holy Creator)

(**Note:** The aspirate consonant *h* alliterates with the vowel *ae*.)

The following lines from "A Ship of Death" (1987), Seamus Heaney's translation of a passage from the Anglo-Saxon epic *Beowulf*, rather loosely follows the accentual meter of the original, occasionally alliterating only two of the stressed syllables, and sometimes introducing two different alliterated sounds in a single line. (I have indicated stressed syllables in bold caps.):

> **SCYLD** was **STILL** a **STRONG** man when his **TIME** came
> and he **CROSSED OV**er into **OUR** Lord's **KEEP**ing.
> **HIS WAR**rior **BAND** did **WHAT** he **BADE** them
> when he **LAID DOWN** the **LAW** among the **DANES**. ...
>
>   (1-4)

So, you may wonder, why should you care about the meter of Anglo-Saxon poetry? Alliterative-stress verse is not much used in English poetry these days, so when it is used it offers the freshness of novelty for both poet and reader, as well as the impact of allusion, which draws into the poem the nuances and implications of Anglo-Saxon verse and the darkly dignified world-view it represents. Besides, when you read those lines aloud, don't you just love the way they sound?

Sound effects are really important in poetry, and we cannot help but respond to the impact of this work's powerful rhythm.

Consider the impact created in the opening sequence of Felicia Dorothea Hemans's "Indian Woman's Death Song" (1828):

> Down a broad river of the western wilds,
> Piercing thick forest-glooms, a light canoe
> Swept with the current: fearful was the speed
> Of the frail bark, as by a tempest's wing
> Borne leaf-like on to where the mist of spray
> Rose with the cataract's thunder. Yet within,
> Proudly, and dauntlessly, and all alone,
> Save that a babe lay sleeping at her breast,
> A woman stood! Upon her Indian brow
> Sat a strange gladness, and her dark hair waved
> As if triumphantly. She pressed her child,
> In its bright slumber, to her beating heart,
> And lifted her sweet voice, that rose awhile
> Above the sound of waters, high and clear,
> Wafting a wild proud strain—a song of death. (1–15)

After a 15-line introductory sequence in a modified version of alliterative-stress meter, the poem changes to accentual-syllabic meter (the kind you are used to hearing in English poetry). The woman's death-song itself, which comprises the rest of the poem, is structured in quatrains rhyming aabb ccdd eeff, and so forth. As in "Junk," the opening sequence in "Indian Woman's Death-Song" borrows its solemnity from the heavy stress pattern of Anglo-Saxon meter.

Many of you are already familiar with the alliterated accentual meter of Anglo-Saxon verse, but if you have not considered it as a possible technique for your own poetry, you might want to go back and give it another look. I also hope those of you who have not really seen alliterative-stress meter in action before might already be thinking of trying it out in your next poem.

Note: The other articles in this series on prosody are "A Beginner's Guide to Prosody"; "A Beginner's Guide to Prosody: Part II (Meter)"; and "A Beginner's Guide to Prosody: Part III (Blank Verse)."

http://tinablue.homestead.com/Prosody4anglosaxonmeter.html

Re-entering into the Poem

When writing about poetry, it is conventional to discuss each poem in technical terms—that is, we want to use the right language to describe the form, the rhythms, the sounds, the structure, the imagery, and so on.

Parts of a Poem

Verse: a single line of poetry.

Stanza: a group of lines, sometimes compared to a paragraph in prose.

Foot: The basic unit of measure in a line of poetry. When we count the number of beats in a line, we are counting the number of feet.

Scansion: (from the Latin *scandere*, "to climb") The practice of climbing up each line of poetry, identifying the stressed and unstressed syllables.

Rhyme: Two or more words that sound alike, contributing patterns of sound in the poem.

Types of Feet

Literary critics have developed elaborate language for writing about rhythm, sound, and meter. It is generally agreed that English poetry employs five basic rhythms of varying stressed (/) and unstressed (x) syllables. The meters are iambs, trochees, spondees, anapests and dactyls. Each unit of rhythm is called a "foot" of poetry.

The meters with two-syllable feet are

Iambic (x /) : "we found (iamb) a shoe (iamb)"
Trochaic (/ x): "David (trochee) Thompson (trochee)"
Spondaic (/ /): "Seeds too (spondee) explode (iamb)"

The meters with three-syllable feet are

Anapestic (x x /): "with a line (anapest) made of blue (anapest)"
Dactylic (/ x x): "sluicing for (dactyl) pieces (trochee) of light (iamb)"

Notice that poetic lines and stanzas are seldom purely iambic or trochaic. Often the poetic effect is achieved through rhythmic variation. Note for example how, in the heroic couplets of Whitman's "O Captain! My Captain!", the iambic meter is interrupted by the five strong spondaic beats that together dramatize the speaker's lament:

/ / / / /
But O heart! heart! heart!
O the bleeding drops of red

In the same poem, the iambic tetrameter rhythm turns quickly into two trochaic beats, with an additional stressed beat added at the end:

x / x / x / x /
Where on the deck my Captain lies,

/ x / x /
Fallen cold and dead.

Types of Rhythm

Rhythm refers to the natural rise and fall of the voice. Each line of a poem, when read aloud, contains a certain number of feet of iambs, trochees, spondees, dactyls or anapests. A line of one foot is a *monometer*, two feet is a *dimeter*, three feet is *trimeter*, four feet is *tetrameter*, five feet is *pentameter*, six feet is *hexameter*, seven feet is *heptameter*, and eight feet is *octameter*. The number of syllables in a line varies therefore according to the meter.

Here's a famous example of iambic tetrameter from Donne's "A Valediction Forbidding Mourning":

x / x / x / x /
So let us melt, and make no noise

The iambic pentameter rhythm adds an additional foot, as in Milton's "On His Blindness":

x / x / x / x / x /
Ere half my days in this dark world and wide

But simply labelling the lines as, say, iambic pentameter, is only the first step in responding technically to a poem. Like a musician, the critic must learn to read and play the notes—to hear the rhythms, vocalize them, and interpret their effects. Meter helps structure the speaking voice, highlighting key phrases and images by varying the verbal emphasis and the pace of the line.

For example, although Marvell's "To His Coy Mistress" is technically written in iambic tetrameter, with eight syllables (four feet) per line, few readers would read it out loud as consistently iambic. Marvell deliberately inserts pauses which break the rhythm, forcing emphasis on key words and images. Indeed, only two lines in the poem present a pure iambic tetrameter rhythm:

$$x \quad / \quad x \ / \ x \ / \ x \quad /$$
The grave's a fine and private place,

$$x \quad / \ x \ / \quad x \ / \quad x \ /$$
But none I think do there embrace.

For another example of rhythm in action, consider the following lines from Kroetsch's poem:

$$x \ / \ x \quad / \quad x \quad / \quad /$$
The fallen roof and fireweed

$$/ \quad /$$
conspire.
$$/ \quad / \ x \quad /$$
  Seeds too explode.
$$/ \ x \ x \quad / \quad / \ x \quad x \ / x$$
Iamb and jackhammer in duet:
$$/ \ x \quad / \quad x \ x \quad /$$
silence, breaking the drum:

$$x \quad / x \quad / \quad x \quad / \quad x$$
the city, climbing, climbing.

These lines balance spondaic emphasis and the regularity of iambic rhythm, both demonstrating and describing "Iamb and jackhammer in duet." The iambic impulse is forward moving, regular and conversational; the spondaic (and the trochaic) calls attention to the present moment, to the immediacy of the landscape.

One of the most famous commentaries on the role of sound in poetry is found in Alexander Pope's "An Essay on Criticism," where the speaker argues that, in a good poem, "the sound must [always] seem an echo to the sense":

> But most by numbers judge a poet's song,
> And smooth or rough, with them, is right or wrong;
> In the bright muse though thousand charms conspire,
> Her voice is all these tuneful fools admire,
> Who haunt Parnassus* but to please their ear,
> Not mend their minds; as some to church repair,
> Not for the doctrine, but the music there.
> These equal syllables alone require,
> Though oft the ear the open vowels tire,
> While expletives their feeble aid do join,
> And ten low words oft creep in one dull line,
> While they ring round the same unvaried chimes,
> With sure returns of still expected rhymes.
> Where'er you find "the cooling western breeze,"
> In the next line, it "whispers through the trees";
> If crystal streams with "pleasing murmurs creep,"
> The reader's threatened (not in vain) with "sleep":
> Then, at the last, and only couplet fraught
> With some unmeaning thing they call a thought,
> A needless Alexandrine† ends the song,
> That like a wounded snake, drags its slow length along.
> Leave such to tune their own dull rhymes, and know
> What's roundly smooth, or languishingly slow;
> And praise the easy vigour of a line,
> Where Denham's strength, and Waller's sweetness join.
> True ease in writing comes from art, not chance,
> As those move easiest who have learned to dance,
> 'Tis not enough no harshness gives offence,
> The sound must seem an echo to the sense:
> Soft is the strain when Zephyr gently blows,
> And the smooth stream in smoother numbers flows;
> But when loud surges lash the sounding shore,
> The hoarse, rough verse should like the torrent roar:
> When Ajax strives, some rock's vast weight to throw,
> The line too labours, and the words move slow;

---

* Parnassus: a Greek mountain associated with the Muses (poetic inspiration).
† Alexandrine: a twelve-syllable line, like line 21.

Not so, when swift Camilla‡ scours the plain,
Flies o'er th'unbending Corn, and skims along the main.

Types of Rhyme

Robert Frost once wrote that "poetry without rhyme is like tennis without a net." Rhyme, like rhythm and meter, provides the poet (and the reader) with a sense of order and pattern—with rules that can be obeyed or resisted. Generally speaking, words are said to rhyme when two or more contain identical or similar vowel sounds and consonant sounds: "a poet's *song*" and "right or *wrong*"; "couplet *fraught*" and "call a *thought*." Rhymes, whether exact (or perfect) or slant-rhymes (imperfect, sharing the same vowel sounds but different consonant sounds), help reinforce patterns of meaning, sound, imagery, and tone. Rhyme draws attention to key words, making phrasing memorable.

| 129 |

Here's an example of a famous slant-rhyme (from the concluding couplet to Shakespeare's Sonnet 116):

If this be error and upon me proved,
I never writ, nor no man ever loved.

Types of Poetic Device

The following devices are used to emphasize key words and images, to scaffold the structure of ideas, to create associations among words and images, to consciously conjoin sound with sense, to adjust the speed of reading, and to generally heighten the musical qualities of poetry. Each of these devices, when used well, encourages us to respond to certain sounds, words, and images as meaningfully associated—and thus the poetic devices contribute meaningful patterning. Like rhythm and rhyme, poetic devices may affect the pace of reading, slowing us down (through, for example, the clustering of discordant sounds) or speeding us up (through, for example, alliteration). While the six devices selected for illustration below by no means exhaust the variety of devices used by poets, they should give you some essential points of departure. No doubt your instructor will want to introduce further devices and examples during your discussions about individual poems.

---

‡ Camilla: a goddess so light of foot that she could skim across the water without getting her feet wet.

alliteration: the repetition of initial consonant sounds. Keats's "Ode on a Grecian Urn" opens with a wonderful mix of alliteration and assonance, where the "s" sounds of "still," "unravished," and "quietness" echo in the alliteration "silence and slow time / Sylvan historian."

> Thou still unravished bride of quietness,
>> Thou foster child of silence and slow time,
> Sylvan historian, who canst thus express
>> A flowery tale more sweetly than our rhyme:

assonance: the repetition of vowel sounds—as illustrated by the long vowel "I," also from Keats's Ode:

> bride of quietness, / Thou foster child of silence and slow time

Here the pairing of vowel sounds subtly draws attention to key words, making them more memorable and encouraging the reader to seek associations and otherwise unspoken connections.

consonance: the repetition of consonant sounds two or more times in short succession, as in the repetition of "t" sounds in the opening three lines of Shakespeare's Sonnet 116:

> Let me not to the marriage of true minds
> Admit impediments. Love is not love
> Which alters when it alteration finds,
> Or bends with the remover to remove:

Like assonance, consonance encourages the reader to associate key words—and it also has the added effect of emphasizing the rhythm or the beat of the poem.

imagery: language that evokes sensory perceptions—sight, sound, taste, touch, and smell. Marvell's "To His Coy Mistress" offers a classic example of a speaker linking imagery to the development of a poetic argument. The images progress from the exotic to the deadened to the passionate. In the final lines of the poem, the speaker combines several image patterns of movement, time, light, and fiery passion, focusing by the poem's end on an image of the sun:

> Let us roll all our strength and all

Our sweetness up into one ball,
And tear our pleasures with rough strife
Thorough the iron gates of life:
Thus, though we cannot make our sun
Stand still, yet we will make him run.

Sometimes, as in Browning's dramatic monologue "My Last Duchess," the poet may use poetic devices sparingly. Imagery in this poem is tied to a painting, a blush on the Duchess's cheek, and a sculpture:

Sir, 'twas not
Her husband's presence only, called that spot
Of joy into the Duchess' cheek: perhaps
Frà Pandolf chanced to say "Her mantle laps
Over my lady's wrist too much," or "Paint
Must never hope to reproduce the faint
Half-flush that dies along her throat": such stuff
Was courtesy, she thought, and cause enough
For calling up that spot of joy.

metaphor: the linking together of unlike objects or ideas. In perhaps the most famous pairing of unlike objects, John Donne's "A Valediction Forbidding Mourning" likens two souls to the two legs of a compass—and extends the metaphor in remarkable ways throughout the poem:

Our two souls therefore, which are one,
   Though I must go, endure not yet
A breach, but an expansion,
   Like gold to airy thinness beat.

If they be two, they are two so
   As stiff twin compasses are two;
Thy soul, the fix'd foot, makes no show
   To move, but doth, if th' other do.

onomatopoeia: the occasions when a word imitates the sound it represents. Words such as "ding dong!" and "crackle" are onomatopoetic. The following line from Pope's "Essay on Criticism" represents in sound what it describes:

> When Ajax strives some rock's vast weight to throw,
> The line too labours, and the words move slow.

Onomatopoeia also refers to words and groupings of words that capture specific sounds. A famous example is Tennyson's representation of a swarm of bees buzzing, in his "Come Down, O Maid":

> The moan of doves in immemorial elms,
> And murmuring of innumerable bees.

Integrating Quotations

Writing about literature always follows the "quote-and-discuss" formula. Sometimes, when writing about a short poem, your instructor may ask you to quote the entire text and then discuss. More often, you will need to integrate quotations (as elegantly as possible) into your essay.

Quoting poetry requires that you become aware of some specific formatting conventions. If quoting fewer than four lines, for example, you should convert the poetic arrangement into a prose form: without changing the capitalization, separate each line by a diagonal slash (/), and indicate the line numbers quoted. For example, lines 26 and 27 of Pope's poem would be quoted in the following manner:

> Pope insists that "True ease in writing comes from art, not chance, / As those move easiest who have learned to dance" (26–27).

When quoting four or more lines, arrange them exactly as they appear in the original poem, indenting the lines as a block quotation and citing the line numbers quoted in parentheses:

> Pope insists that "True ease in writing" poetry is no matter of chance:

> > True ease in writing comes from art, not chance,
> > As those move easiest who have learned to dance,
> > 'Tis not enough no harshness gives offence,
> > The sound must seem an echo to the sense. (26–29)

Note that block quotations do not require quotation marks.

How to Move from an "F" to an "A": Modelling the Process

Understanding the mechanics of poetry helps us appreciate the artistry of the poet's craft; it also gives us something concrete to write about. In this section we will employ the critical tools and go step-by-step through the process of (1) identifying and exploring a critical issue, (2) finding the right approach to develop the issue, and (3) making sure that resolving the issue makes an appropriate contribution to the field. We begin by taking a failing but promising opening paragraph, transforming it into a strong piece of critical writing. Using examples | **133** | from student essays, I'll further demonstrate and discuss the process of successful revision.

The following sample introductions represent an amalgam taken from actual student essays on Kroetsch's poem. They are arranged in ascending order, ranging from unsuccessful to excellent. As you read the student writing, note how the theme of social and physical integration develops from essay to essay. See how the more successful versions contextualize and specify that theme and link it to (1) a particular pattern, and (2), in at least one case, a clear critical issue.

VERSION #1

When looking at the poem "This Part of the Country" the ideas and imagery help Robert Kroetsch write the way that he did. At first this poem seems a confusing story of one man getting lost in the snow during a winter's night. There are many examples of that in the poem. When we look closer we see what the poet is trying to say. I think the poem is more about travel and the effect of the cold on both the man and the landscape, which is the main theme. And by the end of the poem the man has been changed by his experience. He feels more at home.

VERSION #2

Robert Kroetsch's "This Part of the Country" depicts a journey in which the author is transformed from an outsider figure into an integrated element of the landscape. When the author says "Somewhere west and south of Mt Robson I forgot my name," he is reflecting on his experience of needing to let go of where he came from and of his outsider perceptions. As readers we are encouraged to empathize with this sense of transformation, those times when we have let go of our old ways and become more comfortable in a new environment.

Kroetsch, though, literally becomes part of the environment when his shoulders become "slopes for elegant white toboggans" and his fingers "assume the dignity of ice." The "S" sounds of "slopes," "toboggans," "assume," and "ice" link the words and create a slippery winter image. It is through such imagery that Kroetsch moves us from "the simple and impossible task of describing a landscape" to the prospect of inhabiting a new landscape.

VERSION #3

Duality plays a key role in Robert Kroetsch's "This Part of the Country," for in each of the four parts of the poem, images of contradiction mark the speaker's transition from isolated individual to integrated community member. Part One establishes the initial point of arrival, where each contrasting element only exacerbates the speaker's feelings of dislocation. Yet even here the image of "Two rivers … coming together" hints subtly of a possible integration with both landscape and community. Part Two juxtaposes the names of explorers and writers, suggesting perhaps that all writers are, by nature, explorers—and that the process of physical exploration is a prerequisite to successfully knowing any new place. Part Three, entitled "Blue River: Checking In" takes the otherwise banal notion of checking into a hotel and introduces a new notion of checking into landscape, history, and culture: here imagery of snow and invisibility, day and night, mark the speaker's transformation from tourist to permanent resident. Similarly, the pace of the poem increases, moving toward the less structured movement of prose poetry. Part Four concludes both the poem and the journey, for here the speaker becomes one with the landscape, his shoulders becoming "slopes for elegant white toboggans" and his feet becoming truly rooted in this new place. Only then, at the poem's end, can the speaker use the words "in this part of the country" like a local: he becomes someone truly "located and dislocated," but the sense of dislocation now takes on positive meaning. By letting go of his self-identification as an outsider figure, the speaker gains an insider's perspective. Where initially the new community's landscape is read like a map, something to be held at arm's length, "a diagram of the impossible," by the poem's end landscape has become something to inhabit, a place of possibilities.

VERSION #4

Robert Kroetsch's "This Part of the Country" explores the complexities and inherent ironies of a "visiting writer-in-residence" reading and writing himself into a new community. Both "visitor" and "resident," the speaker must straddle two worlds: he is someone newly "located but [also] dislocated." Such feelings of ambivalence and contradiction help structure the poem and describe, as Kroetsch explains in an interview, "'a western landscape' where prose and poetry speak to each other, give each other sustenance and inspiration, at once collide and invigorate." This sense of ambivalence, located in the juxtaposition of movement and stasis, informs the poem's rhythms, diction, and narrative; this is a place where, in the poem's opening observations, the landscape speaks in an initially foreign, even conspiratorial, tongue:

> The fallen roof and fireweed
> conspire.
>
>   Seeds too explode.
> Iamb and jackhammer in duet:
>
> silence, breaking the drum:
> the city, climbing, climbing.

The explosive, spondaic energy in these lines is balanced against an underlying iambic rhythm: as the speaker says, the landscape reveals "Iamb and jackhammer in duet." The iambs move us forward; the jackhammer spondees and trochees hold us back. Similarly, the soft "c" and "s" sounds are linked to a meditative forward motion, while the explosive "p" and "b" sounds (and the hard "k" of "jackhammer" and "breaking") make meditation impossible. The landscape arrests the speaker's attention—and ours. Most arresting of all is the casual phrase that gives the poem its title: "this part of the country" suggests the kind of assumed ownership and secure local knowledge that the speaker envies but does not initially share; but it also gives him a point of entry, a renewed faith in the power of language to, in time, move him closer to describing the ineffable. Poetry, like the landscape, "is a diagram of the impossible," for just as we "have to look at trees to see the wind," we must use words to speak the unspeakable. "This Part of the Country" is at once a travel poem and an arrival poem that carefully blurs easy distinctions between what is lost and what is found, what is absent and what is present, what is unspoken and what can be heard.

Commentary

Each version does some things well, but as the comments below indicate, the versions are not equally successful as samples of critical writing.

Version #1 gives us the gist of the poem, and provides a typical first draft. It offers a tentative focus on the theme of change, indicating that the speaker moves from feeling lost and isolated to feeling one with the landscape. The author's textual stance seems very general, the institutional stance is not yet secure (that is, the author has not yet mastered the conventions of writing a critical essay), and the field stance has not been invoked at all. This introduction shows promise, but, at this point, it is little more than an abbreviated plot summary. Notice also that by using the phrase "what the poet is trying to say," the student seems to suggest that Kroetsch is unable to communicate clearly—a reading that would likely irritate many instructors and poets. Perhaps most significantly, the author is not yet employing the "quote-and-discuss" formula typical of critical writing. Grammatically and stylistically, this introduction needs further work: the opening sentence shows a modification error (the "ideas and imagery" are not doing the "looking"); the word "that" in sentence 3 provides an unclear reference; and the overall organization needs a guiding thesis. Most instructors would rate this writing in the F to D range.

Version #2 is much more direct and focused, and quotations are beginning to be used as textual support. The social stance ("As readers we …") seems strong, as does the textual stance (with the attention to sounds and imagery); but the writing lacks the field stance (the use of critical questions, approaches, and insights drawn from secondary sources). Here the theme of change receives some detailed commentary, with clear transitions ("Kroetsch, though, literally becomes …" and "It is through such imagery that …") between ideas. The final sentence offers an excellent foundation for a strong essay. Grammatically and stylistically, this introduction shows greater confidence than version #1. The second sentence, though, needs considerable revision: at present the large number of prepositions ("of," "on," "of," "to," "of," and "in") tends to clutter the sentence, creating confusion. As a general rule, sentences containing more than two or three prepositions require revision. Most instructors would rate this writing in the C+ to B– range.

In Version #3 the student opens with a general critical issue ("duality") and links the issue immediately to what she sees as the poem's theme ("the speaker's transition from isolated individual to integrated community member"). This version's strength lies with its logical structure, clear organization, and effective use of quotations as textual support. The critical issue could be clarified further—that is, the author could define in specific terms how duality works at multiple levels within the poem (thematically, linguistically, figuratively, and so on). The focus on duality, on images of contradiction, gets a little lost when the author introduces references to explorers, the hotel, and the landscape; the writing regains focus when the author returns to issues of location and dislocation. In summary, quotations are used as evidence to support the interpretation, the writing is clear, and we get a strong sense of where the argument is going. This introduction shows a much more secure understanding of the social, textual, and field stances than either version #1 or version #2. Most instructors would rate writing like this in the B to B+ range.

Version #4 displays extraordinary confidence and control. The student draws upon the interview to help contextualize a reading of the work. We learn that the experience of the speaker and the poet are closely aligned, and that knowing about Kroetsch's role as a "visiting writer-in-residence" contributes significantly to our understanding of the poem. In this version the pattern of contradictions and dualities is given clear definition and remains the essay's clear point of focus; in addition, the pattern is linked to the poem's theme and helps establish a critical issue: it tells us something new (i.e., of interest to the field) about Kroetsch's ambivalence toward movement and stasis in both his life and his poetry. Like version #3, the student uses quotations effectively, but in this version the student lingers over key passages, offering detailed technical discussion. The poem's rhythm, diction, and narrative are, for this student, clearly interconnected; and the introduction's final sentence promises an organized explication of these interconnections. Some readers might object to the density of the writing, for the author certainly packs a lot into a single paragraph. The author could, for example, break the introduction into two paragraphs, beginning a paragraph #2 with "Most arresting of all is the casual phrase ...." That said, most instructors would recognize this writing as superior work, rating it in the A to A+ range.

Box 5.2: Field Notes from a Writing Teacher:
Thirteen Ways of Thinking about a Poem

Writing about Poetry

David Wilson-Okamura

Thirteen things to think about while you're planning your papers:

1. Robert Frost once defined poetry as "what gets lost in translation." What is the difference between this poem and a prose paraphrase of this poem?

2. Write about what the poem accomplishes beyond its prose meaning. How do images, rhythms, patterns, and repeated phrases modify or extend the prose meaning of the poem?

3. Notice that I said "how": all poetry has images, rhythm, pattern, and repetition; the fact that a given poem has these things is true, but not interesting. Write instead about the way that these things are used: do they enhance the prose meaning of the poem? qualify it? undercut it? etc. Another way to put the same question: what is the relationship between the content of this poem and its form?

4. Don't let your paper turn into a laundry list of observations. Make sure that no one could title your paper "Some Things I Liked about This Poem." Both of these things are a sure recipe for a C.

5. A recipe for avoiding the laundry-list phenomenon: After you've gone through the poem for yourself, noticing things and making notes, ask yourself "What is the total effect of all the little things I've been noticing?" What do the parts of the poem cooperate to mean? When you've answered this question to your own satisfaction, you're ready to start writing your paper.

6. Since you now know what you want to say, organize your observations in such a way as to communicate this to someone who doesn't already know what you think, and who may even disagree with you when he or she does! Remember the evil laundry list. Some ways to organize your observations: types of imagery, themes, patterns, repeated words; there are lots more. Suggestion: Whenever you take up a new topic (say, the compass image in Donne's "Valediction Forbidding Mourning"), be sure to relate that topic to the total effect of the poem. You can do this when you introduce the topic, or you can do this when you finish talking about the topic, but don't forget to do it.

7. How should you start a paper then? Let me make a suggestion. Instead of telling your reader why you like the poem you've chosen to write about, start your paper with a question or a problem: "What makes this poem hard to understand (or hard to like)?" It may be a single line; it may be a set of lines; it may be an attitude, or a category of images. Work outward from there. How would the poem be different if it didn't have this problem? Most importantly, what does the problem tell you about the poem as a whole? Remember, your job is not to say how great a given poem is or tell your reader how much you liked it. These things go without saying (why would you spend time writing a paper about a bad poem?), so don't say them.

8. When you are explaining what an image means or suggests, ground your explanation in the text itself. It's not enough to say that image x makes you think of experience y. Say *why* such-and-such an image suggests such-and-such an idea; appeals to personal associations are not usually very convincing, so it's best to omit them and ground your inferences instead on the words themselves.

9. What does it mean to ground your inferences in the words of the text? Here's a tip: Ask yourself, "How is the poet guiding me to think about the objects in the poem? Are there other images or words in the poem that corroborate my interpretation of this particular word or image?"

10. If you decide that you need to do some research on a poem or author, do so. Remember, though, that your goal is to gather evidence for an argument about a poem. If, for instance, you decide that the poet's biography is relevant to your argument about the poem, then tell your reader about the relevant facts. Do not, however, pad your essay with random facts.

11. Don't summarize your argument with a quotation from the critics. Doing so makes it sound as if you have nothing to add. (Sometimes, of course, that's how one feels: what is there left to say? When this happens, see the following suggestion.)

12. If you must cite a literary critic, build on what she says, don't build up to it. Use the observations of your predecessors as building

139

blocks. When you find that someone has already said what you wanted to say, don't despair. Congratulate yourself on the fact that you, as an undergraduate, have seen something that it took a grey-haired professor decades to discover, and move on. Instead of despairing ("Oh no! I have nothing left to say!"), wipe your hands, breathe a sigh of relief ("Well, that's one less thing for me to do—I can just tell my reader to 'see Peabody, pp. 29–37'") and move on. Push the argument a step further. If x is true, what does that say about y? Stand on the shoulders of the giants! See farther!

13. Or ignore the critics altogether and reread the poem.

Complete Texts for the Poems Referenced in This Chapter

Sonnet 116

Let me not to the marriage of true minds
Admit impediments. Love is not love
Which alters when it alteration finds,
Or bends with the remover to remove:
O, no! it is an ever-fixèd mark,   5
That looks on tempests and is never shaken;
It is the star to every wand'ring bark,
Whose worth's unknown, although his height be taken.
Love's not Time's fool, though rosy lips and cheeks
Within his bending sickle's compass come;   10
Love alters not with his brief hours and weeks,
But bears it out even to the edge of doom.
    If this be error and upon me proved,
    I never writ, nor no man ever loved.

William Shakespeare (1564–1616)

A Valediction Forbidding Mourning

As virtuous men pass mildly away,
    And whisper to their souls to go,
Whilst some of their sad friends do say
    "Now his breath goes," and some say, "No."

So let us melt, and make no noise,   5
    No tear-floods, nor sigh-tempests move ;
'Twere profanation of our joys
    To tell the laity our love.

Moving of th' earth brings harms and fears ;
    Men reckon what it did, and meant ;   10
But trepidation of the spheres,
    Though greater far, is innocent.

| 141 |

Dull sublunary lovers' love
    —Whose soul is sense—cannot admit
Of absence, 'cause it doth remove   15
    The thing which elemented it.

But we by a love so much refined,
    That ourselves know not what it is,
Inter-assurèd of the mind,
    Care less, eyes, lips and hands to miss.   20

Our two souls therefore, which are one,
    Though I must go, endure not yet
A breach, but an expansion,
    Like gold to airy thinness beat.

If they be two, they are two so   25
    As stiff twin compasses are two ;
Thy soul, the fix'd foot, makes no show
To move, but doth, if th' other do.

And though it in the centre sit,
    Yet, when the other far doth roam,   30
It leans, and hearkens after it,
    And grows erect, as that comes home.

Such wilt thou be to me, who must,
    Like th' other foot, obliquely run;
Thy firmness makes my circle just,   35
    And makes me end where I begun.

John Donne (1572–1631)

On His Blindness

When I consider how my light is spent
   Ere half my days in this dark world and wide,
   And that one talent which is death to hide
   Lodg'd with me useless, though my soul more bent
To serve therewith my Maker, and present
   My true account, lest he returning chide,
   "Doth God exact day-labour, light denied?"
   I fondly ask. But Patience, to prevent
That murmur, soon replies: "God doth not need
   Either man's work or his own gifts: who best
   Bear his mild yoke, they serve him best. His state
Is kingly; thousands at his bidding speed
   And post o'er land and ocean without rest:
   They also serve who only stand and wait."

John Milton (1608–74)

To His Coy Mistress

Had we but world enough and time,
This coyness, lady, were no crime.
We would sit down and think which way
To walk, and pass our long love's day.
Thou by the Indian Ganges' side
Should'st rubies find; I by the tide
Of Humber would complain. I would
Love you ten years before the Flood,
And you should, if you please, refuse
Till the conversion of the Jews.
My vegetable love should grow
Vaster than empires, and more slow.
An hundred years should go to praise
Thine eyes, and on thy forehead gaze;
Two hundred to adore each breast,
But thirty thousand to the rest.
An age at least to every part,
And the last age should show your heart.
For, lady, you deserve this state,
Nor would I love at lower rate.

But at my back I always hear
Time's wingèd chariot hurrying near;
And yonder all before us lie
Deserts of vast eternity.
Thy beauty shall no more be found,
Nor in thy marble vault shall sound
My echoing song; then worms shall try
That long-preserved virginity,
And your quaint honor turn to dust,
And into ashes all my lust.
The grave's a fine and private place,
But none, I think, do there embrace.
Now therefore, while the youthful hue
Sits on thy skin like morning dew,
And while thy willing soul transpires
At every pore with instant fires,
    Now let us sport us while we may,
And now, like amorous birds of prey,
Rather at once our time devour
Than languish in his slow-chapped power.
Let us roll all our strength and all
Our sweetness up into one ball,
And tear our pleasures with rough strife
Thorough the iron gates of life.
Thus, though we cannot make our sun
Stand still, yet we will make him run.

Andrew Marvell (1621–78)

Ode on a Grecian Urn

Thou still unravished bride of quietness,
    Thou foster child of silence and slow time,
Sylvan historian, who canst thus express
    A flowery tale more sweetly than our rhyme:
What leaf-fringed legend haunts about thy shape
    Of deities or mortals, or of both,
        In Tempe or the dales of Arcady?
    What men or gods are these? What maidens loath?
What mad pursuit? What struggle to escape?
        What pipes and timbrels? What wild ecstasy?

Heard melodies are sweet, but those unheard
   Are sweeter; therefore, ye soft pipes, play on;
Not to the sensual ear, but, more endeared,
   Pipe to the spirit ditties of no tone:
Fair youth, beneath the trees, thou canst not leave
   Thy song, nor ever can those trees be bare;
     Bold Lover, never, never canst thou kiss,
Though winning near the goal—yet, do not grieve;
     She cannot fade, though thou hast not thy bliss
   Forever wilt thou love, and she be fair!

Ah, happy, happy boughs! that cannot shed
   Your leaves, nor ever bid the Spring adieu;
And, happy melodist, unwearièd,
   For ever piping songs for ever new;
More happy love! more happy, happy love!
   Forever warm and still to be enjoyed,
     Forever panting, and forever young;
All breathing human passion far above,
   That leaves a heart high-sorrowful and cloyed,
     A burning forehead, and a parching tongue.

Who are these coming to the sacrifice?
   To what green altar, O mysterious priest,
Lead'st thou that heifer lowing at the skies,
   And all her silken flanks with garlands dressed?
What little town by river or sea shore,
   Or mountain-built with peaceful citadel,
     Is emptied of this folk, this pious morn?
And, little town, thy streets for evermore
   Will silent be; and not a soul to tell
     Why thou art desolate, can e'er return.

O Attic shape! Fair attitude! with brede
   Of marble men and maidens overwrought,
With forest branches and the trodden weed;
   Thou, silent form, dost tease us out of thought
As doth eternity: Cold Pastoral!
   When old age shall this generation waste,
     Thou shalt remain, in midst of other woe
   Than ours, a friend to man, to whom thou say'st,

"Beauty is truth, truth beauty,"—that is all
    Ye know on earth, and all ye need to know.

      John Keats (1795–1821)

My Last Duchess
Ferrara

That's my last duchess painted on the wall,
Looking as if she were alive. I call
That piece a wonder, now; Frà Pandolf's hands
Worked busily a day, and there she stands.
Will't please you sit and look at her? I said
"Frà Pandolf" by design, for never read
Strangers like you that pictured countenance,
The depth and passion of its earnest glance,
But to myself they turned (since none puts by
The curtain I have drawn for you, but I)
And seemed as they would ask me, if they durst,
How such a glance came there; so, not the first
Are you to turn and ask thus. Sir, 'twas not
Her husband's presence only, called that spot
Of joy into the Duchess' cheek; perhaps
Frà Pandolf chanced to say "Her mantle laps
Over my lady's wrist too much," or "Paint
Must never hope to reproduce the faint
Half-flush that dies along her throat." Such stuff
Was courtesy, she thought, and cause enough
For calling up that spot of joy. She had
A heart—how shall I say?—too soon made glad,
Too easily impressed; she liked whate'er
She looked on, and her looks went everywhere.
Sir, 'twas all one! My favor at her breast,
The dropping of the daylight in the West,
The bough of cherries some officious fool
Broke in the orchard for her, the white mule
She rode with round the terrace—all and each
Would draw from her alike the approving speech,
Or blush, at least. She thanked men—good! but thanked
Somehow—I know not how—as if she ranked
My gift of a nine-hundred-years-old name

With anybody's gift. Who'd stoop to blame
This sort of trifling? Even had you skill
In speech—which I have not—to make your will
Quite clear to such an one, and say, "Just this
Or that in you disgusts me; here you miss,
Or there exceed the mark"—and if she let
Herself be lessoned so, nor plainly set
Her wits to yours, forsooth, and make excuse
—E'en then would be some stooping; and I choose
Never to stoop. Oh sir, she smiled, no doubt,
Whene'er I passed her; but who passed without
Much the same smile? This grew; I gave commands;
Then all smiles stopped together. There she stands
As if alive. Will't please you rise? We'll meet
The company below, then. I repeat,
The Count your master's known munificence
Is ample warrant that no just pretense
Of mine for dowry will be disallowed;
Though his fair daughter's self, as I avowed
At starting, is my object. Nay, we'll go
Together down, sir. Notice Neptune, though,
Taming a sea-horse, thought a rarity,
Which Claus of Innsbruck cast in bronze for me!

Robert Browning (1812–89)

Come Down, O Maid

Come down, O maid, from yonder mountain height:
What pleasure lives in height (the shepherd sang),
In height and cold, the splendour of the hills?
But cease to move so near the Heavens, and cease
To glide a sunbeam by the blasted Pine,
To sit a star upon the sparkling spire;
And come, for Love is of the valley, come,
For Love is of the valley, come thou down
And find him; by the happy threshold, he,
Or hand in hand with Plenty in the maize,
Or red with spirted purple of the vats,
Or foxlike in the vine; nor cares to walk
With Death and Morning on the silver horns,

Nor wilt thou snare him in the white ravine,
Nor find him dropt upon the firths of ice,
That huddling slant in furrow-cloven falls
To roll the torrent out of dusky doors:
But follow; let the torrent dance thee down
To find him in the valley; let the wild
Lean-headed Eagles yelp alone, and leave
The monstrous ledges there to slope, and spill
Their thousand wreaths of dangling water-smoke,
That like a broken purpose waste in air:
So waste not thou; but come; for all the vales
Await thee; azure pillars of the hearth
Arise to thee; the children call, and I
Thy shepherd pipe, and sweet is every sound,
Sweeter thy voice, but every sound is sweet;
Myriads of rivulets hurrying thro' the lawn,
The moan of doves in immemorial elms,
And murmuring of innumerable bees.

Alfred Lord Tennyson (1809–92)

O Captain! My Captain!

O Captain! my Captain! our fearful trip is done,
The ship has weather'd every rack, the prize we sought is won,
The port is near, the bells I hear, the people all exulting,
While follow eyes the steady keel, the vessel grim and daring;
    But O heart! heart! heart!
        O the bleeding drops of red,
            Where on the deck my Captain lies,
                Fallen cold and dead.

O Captain! my Captain! rise up and hear the bells;
Rise up—for you the flag is flung—for you the bugle trills,
For you bouquets and ribbon'd wreaths—for you the shores
a-crowding,
For you they call, the swaying mass, their eager faces turning;
    Here Captain! dear father!
        This arm beneath your head!
            It is some dream that on the deck,
                You've fallen cold and dead.

My Captain does not answer, his lips are pale and still,
My father does not feel my arm, he has no pulse nor will,
The ship is anchor'd safe and sound, its voyage closed and done,
From fearful trip the victor ship comes in with object won;
  Exult O shores, and ring O bells!
  But I with mournful tread,
    Walk the deck my Captain lies,
     Fallen cold and dead.

Walt Whitman (1819–92)

Chapter 6

Some Final Words on Writing about Literature

Four Critics Speak on Their Personal Approaches to Critical Writing

W̶e conclude with four brief narratives, each addressing the process of writing literary criticism. Like Professor Harold Kolb, Jr., each critic uses a variety of approaches, seeking the kind of "principled opportunism" that Kolb advances. While the various approaches may provide us with a tool kit for reading literature, the choice of those tools varies from critic to critic. These narratives offer a valuable reminder that, however complex and detached it may seem, the writing of critical essays remains a highly personal activity. Each of the following represents a response to the question, "What critical approach (or approaches) do you use, and what methods does this approach involve?"

Alice Farley, Professor of English, Southern Illinois University at Edwardsville

In my 30 years as a college-level teacher, I have lived with a stressful, but ultimately inspiring, classroom habit: I find myself asking my students a question about an assigned text without having thought through the answer in advance. In the case of "The Bride Comes to Yellow Sky," I recall asking my students why the bride had no name. With considerable prompting, I got them to answer that one. But then, as usual, I went too far, asking if they could rationalize the other names in the story. They couldn't; so I ended up free associating and brainstorming explanations as I went along. The more I spoke (babbled, actually), the more I sensed the topic's potential as a brief scholarly essay.

So I went home and jotted down the ideas that had somehow emerged during my classroom performance. (I find that I must write them down while they're still fresh. Otherwise, most of them disappear assuredly as dreams disappear.) I then searched the MLA bibliography to compile a list of scholarly essays devoted to "The Bride Comes to Yellow Sky," noting with triumph that no one seemed to have mined my topic already. I tracked down and photocopied each of the essays. I then tracked down every book on Crane in the Brown University library. I took notes on each essay, and on the passages in the books that seemed to be potentially useful. I also took notes on the story itself. Each note—a single quotation or a single idea—was written on its own 4x6 index card, with a code for the source in the upper left-hand corner. (Usually, material from the text being analyzed ends up on white cards; material from secondary sources goes on yellow cards.) This part of the writing process, which easily could generate dozens of note cards, is admittedly time- and labour-intensive; but, as with painting a room, preparation is three-fourths of the work.

Once I had all my index cards ready, I read through them. Some cards suddenly seemed of question-able usefulness; those were set aside. With the retained cards, however, patterns emerged quickly: some cards seemed to go together naturally, so they were placed in their respective piles with post-it notes as labels (e.g., "Scratchy"). (The piles usually were arranged on the living-room floor. Larger projects, like books, require additional rooms.) Very soon, the piles themselves seemed to assume ideational patterns, so I rearranged them accordingly. By the time I'd finished, it was obvious that the rearranged piles would correspond, in order, to different sections of my essay. In effect, the note cards had determined the arrangement of my arguments and the structure of the essay itself.

The next difficult part was writing the opening paragraph. I am well aware that this is the single most important part of an essay, since it should present the thesis while giving the reader an overview of the physical/intellectual arrangement of the essay. Usually I can compose the opening paragraph mentally while pacing the floor. If that fails, I take a nap to let my subconscious work on it, being sure to concentrate on the embryonic essay while falling asleep. When I wake up, the opening is usually very clear, so I write it down quickly—and I do mean write it down: until quite recently, I have done all my scholarly writing (some 50 essays and five books) in longhand, using a blue ballpoint pen on lined paper. (I always draw in large margins in faint pencil, to facilitate editing.) Once the opening is on paper, the rest of the essay essentially writes itself.

Basically, I work through one pile of cards after another; the words just seem to flow out, while unexpected ideas and connections keep material-izing. If I can't think of a word fast enough, I don't waste time on it; I leave a blank space on the paper, and fill it in later, during editing. (As I work in quotations and ideas from the note cards, I set them aside in a new card pile labelled "Endnotes.") Once I've finished, I set the draft aside, ideally for several days, and try not to think about it. Then I go over it again. The editing is time-consuming and a little messy: using pens in different colours (usually black and red), I will add or delete a few sentences, replace one word with a more precise one, craft clearer transitions, and so on. Then I type it up, doing a bit more editing in the process. Next, because I'm terrible at naming things, I usually ask someone to read the essay and think up a title for it. (Luckily for me, *The Explicator* used the title of the story in lieu of an original one.)

By the way, whenever I read an essay or book of mine several years after publication, it always seems as if it were written by someone else. That used to bother me. Now it just seems one of the more mysterious aspects of the writing process.

Katherine Sutherland, Associate Professor of English, Thompson Rivers University

I write from my belly, and I mean this in a nearly literal way. When I was 18 and just starting university, I found feminists appalling—they were so, well, socially unattractive, and I was far more interested in getting a boyfriend than in declaring open allegiance to the sisterhood of unshaved underarms. Who needed feminists, anyhow, I asked myself, as men and women were pretty much equal already? But after my BA, I left school for two years to work as a telephone operator, perhaps the most oppressively female job one might have, and I learned that the contrived equity of the ivory tower does not extend beyond the university campus—and

now that I am a professor, I recognize that even the academy contains embedded inequities for all kinds of people. Thus, when I returned to university to do a Master's degree, I became obsessed with body theory, that is, the study of how bodies are socially constructed. I wanted to account for inequities between bodies; I began to understand language as a body, grammar as skeleton, signification as blood. Now, I write from my belly, and it is sometimes a painful process.

Ever notice how many people (like Alice Farley in this book) compare writing to birth? Well, one thing any mother knows is that no two labours are ever exactly the same, but they always involve some degree of suffering. Usually when I write, I begin with an idea, something invisible and deep inside me, something that grows slowly even when I am not consciously thinking about it. Careful of this idea, I begin to read, promiscuously and rather randomly, anything that seems related, seeking the strange collisions of unlikely texts. After some weeks, or months, or even years (depending on the length of explanation the idea will sustain), my brain feels bloated, ponderous, ready. This distressing state lasts until I realize, very abruptly, how things fit together—and then I realize that my reading wasn't random at all, that mysterious and private things were working together inside me to produce meaning whole. Next, I begin to bang away at the computer until my brain is eased of its burden, at which point I stop writing and make a detailed outline at last. Here, I actually begin to enjoy the writing: my idea is outside me now; I can see it, get to know it better, help to form it into an independent thing that doesn't need me anymore. Once my idea sets out into the world—"publish" having the same etymological root as "public"—the process begins again. There are always more ideas waiting to be born, and it is worth remembering that although pregnancy and childbirth are unpleasant, when all is said and done, you have produced something to make you proud.

Michael Jarrett, Professor of English, Penn State University

The Baptist churches that I faithfully attended as a child growing up in Georgia and Tennessee taught me close reading. Week after week and verse by verse, our pastors explicated scripture. Whole hours were spent scrutinizing clauses and phrases in minute detail. The best sermons were dramas: after great labour, ambiguity was banished so that the light of clarity could shine on us all. Interpretation mattered. Our reason for living and our prospects of eternity hung on the meanings of Hebrew, Greek, and English words. And so in graduate school (my BA is in psychology) I discovered that accepted methods of reading great literature were absolutely familiar to me. I recognized them from church.

My pastors had been, more or less, bible-thumping New Critics. Or rather, I came to regard my close-reading professors as ministers in a secular institution: the university. They revered the canonical texts they taught, handling them like holy writ. And their hermeneutics—the interpretative strategies they brought to the work of exposition—clearly derived from methods codified in the Middle Ages (methods that regarded scripture as readable on literal, allegorical, moral, and anagogical levels). Sure, the stakes of literary interpretation were substantially lower than what I'd experienced in church. Misread Melville, and you might lose face; misread St. John, and you could lose your soul.

And this bothered me. I wondered, "What's gained by poring over the words of Shakespeare, Wordsworth, or Faulkner?" My answer arrived when I began to lose faith in the power and privilege of close reading. I'm not going to relate how that happened (the process was "over-determined," Freud would say). Instead, I'll make a declaration: I came to believe that no critical practice is disinterested. Reading is a political act.

Obviously, this is an article of faith, an axiom. It's pragmatic, not provable. It led me to stop worrying about discovering right interpretations, and it prompted me to ask meta-questions: "What sort of agenda, world-view, or ideology is bolstered by a close reading of, say, William Faulkner or Stephen Crane?"

"What are the political uses of literary criticism, especially when it seems most neutral, rational, and objective?" "How are truth effects generated?" Politicizing the process of reading also made me recall some nearly forgotten sermons. My dad hated them. "They're proof texts," he'd say. Their creators used a passage to deliver a point of their own devising, instead of eloquently making manifest a point that was formerly latent. Except for insisting that all ministers employed passages to make points—some were just more bald-faced, less sophisticated than others—I generally agreed with Dad.

That's generally. There were some sermons that moved from close reading to a surprising but apt thesis, and when they concluded, I was left to marvel. Had I heard something found (interpreted like a classical musician reads a score) or something made (invented like a jazz musician improvises a melody)? No matter. That was the effect I most wanted my critical writing to achieve: heuretics. That's what Gregory Ulmer calls the textual orientation that pushes interpretation into the realm of invention. It's an old theological term, but it describes the reading practices employed by post-structuralist writers such as Jacques Derrida and Roland Barthes, writers who express themselves creatively as well as analytically.

There's no formula for working heuretically, but there are surefire ways to get started. I begin by digging into a text. I read closely, follow the rules of New Criticism. But then, typically, I seize on a word or phrase; often it's a marginal item (as opposed to a salient feature). Or better, some word or phrase seizes me, and I investigate how it actually explains what I'm studying. For example, these days I'm obsessed with "ear training" in music and literature. So I use the word "train" and all the associated metaphors (and puns) as a way to explore my topic. I'm obsessed with locomotives, tracks, and gauge (with Crane's "Great Pullman" pulling Western men and women into the future?)—and with pieces of music such as Pierre Schaeffer's "Étude aux Chemins de Fer" and Chessie's *Signal Series*. I believe they'll teach me what I need to know: both how to get thinking "on track" and how to "derail" it.

Nietzsche wrote something like "behind every concept there's a mobile army of metaphors." Heuretics demands that I ride the metaphorical vehicle that gives rise to concepts and see where it will take me. It recommends that I yield to language—follow the logic of association and signification.

Helen Gilbert, Professor of Theatre, Royal Holloway, University of London

Like all literary criticism, post-colonial analysis is a form of detective work that puts the reader in the role of sleuth. But because he/she generally interprets texts in the interests of disenfranchised groups, the

| 153 |

post-colonial sleuth adopts a partisan approach for political purposes.

For me, that means investigating the material effects of a text—how it participates in cultural struggles, how it can be made to serve specific agendas, either openly or tacitly. Whether I am reading a futuristic fantasy or a quasi-autobiographical fiction, I assume that all texts are historically located: that they speak in particular modes to the anxieties and/or aspirations of a particular culture at a specific moment in time. My first interpretive task, then, is to imagine some of the possible relations between a text and its contexts. This is where I find research invaluable, not because it gives me a clear-cut answer but because it defines reasonable limits for my own speculation.

I'm seldom systematic or exhaustive in such research, and I don't confine it to so-called factual data. I allow my curiosity to drive the work, even if that means pursuing an obscure hunch or a seemingly irrelevant footnote. Reviewing the text in the light of my research, I look not only for correspondences but also for gaps and absences, for the pieces that don't seem to fit the puzzle. I don't take anything at face value at this stage. Instead, I assume that the relationships between a text and its various cultural, literary, and political contexts are likely to be complex, even contradictory. A seemingly wayward detail, perhaps a narrative inconsistency or an odd figure of speech, can supply the frisson that suddenly opens up a compelling line of inquiry. I regard such details as forensic evidence of the many stories that might be hidden in the text, not least of which are the muted testimonies of colonized peoples and the forms of censorship (and self-censorship) that they often write within.

When I eventually craft my findings into a critical essay, I assemble both the textual and contextual evidence in ways that support my case, however that has evolved. And while I aim for clarity and consistency in my arguments, I also strive to express myself in artful prose since, at the end of the day, it is often the tremendous power of rhetoric that wins sway over uncertain and elusive "truths."

Language Use in English Studies

Within the discipline of English studies a number of words, expressions, and key metaphors are used with a somewhat different connotation or in a grammatically different way from their common use elsewhere. The following is a partial list of some language usage peculiar to the field of literary criticism.

What follows should in no way be confused with dictionaries or glossaries of literary terminology. The terms "metaphor" and "iambic pentameter," for example, are important for any student of English to know, but these terms are employed within the discipline in very much the same way in which they are employed outside it. The verb "theorize," on the other hand, is commonly used within the discipline of English studies with a direct object, whereas outside the discipline most people speak of theorizing "about" something. We see similar phenomena with the other points of usage listed below.

aestheticize: Much recent critical commentary has refocused attention on the material, social, historical, and political conditions of producing and reading texts—on how books are published, edited, distributed, read, etc. Those critics not interested in such material concerns tend to consider literature as more properly an aesthetic subject, as something removed from the material world. An extreme version of aestheticization occurs when a reader is said to turn the text into a kind of "fetish." *Example:* "By aestheticizing the text and ignoring the role of marriage as a catalyst for change, the critic effectively ignores the bride's historical significance."

appropriate (verb): Until relatively recently, writers from the dominant culture felt free to appropriate the voices of Aboriginal peoples without exciting controversy. Today, most writers (and readers) are more conscious of charges of "stealing" stories or speaking in voices that aim to represent characters from other cultures. *Example:* "For most people in the critical community, the question of appropriating voices and stories is really a question of respect for other cultures and races."

colonization (of meaning and texts): By analogy to the more common historical meaning of the word, meaning is said to be "colonized" or naturalized when it is made to conform to patterns of the dominant culture. The use of this word suggests a recognition of political power as an important element in interpretation. *Example:* "Toward the end of the story, Wilson's faltering attempts at polite language suggest the subtle effects of linguistic colonization."

construct (with a person or people as the direct object): The rise of the word "construct" is almost certainly tied to the twentieth-century philosophical notion that meaning is socially constructed—that individuals, cultures, and narratives are composed socially via interaction with a variety of forces. *Example:* "It is important to understand how Potter and his bride are constructed through visual as well as narrative strategies."

contextualize: The impulse to consider interpretations "in context" derives from the understanding that both contexts and texts affect the way we read. Formalist and many reader-response critics tend to focus on the immediate context of the reading situation, while cultural critics will want to consider multiple and competing contexts for meaning. *Example:* "Our understanding of an outsider figure such as Scratchy Wilson is best contextualized by reference to the outlaw in Western myth and folklore."

discourse (with a meaning rather wider than that of "conversation"): Discourse, as used in this book, refers to the language, traditions, conventions, assumptions, and power relations that define any identifiable language community or text. *Example:* "As teachers of literature, we have a responsibility to highlight the discourse structures that define our discipline."

foreground (as a verb): Literary critics seem to have adopted the term from the visual arts, where notions of foreground and background reflect pictorial traditions of representation and perspective. *Example:* "Stephen Crane's narrative foregrounds the opposition between Eastern technology and Western ritual."

implicate (without any suggestion of a crime having been committed): The word "implicate" (tied closely to reader-response criticism) suggests some measure of responsibility on the part of the reader, where the reader's role is considered important in the "construction" of meaning.

Example: "The passenger's 'wink' implicates us as co-conspirators (accomplices or, at least, fellow Easterners) in judging Potter and his bride on board the train."

legitimize (as a verb): While the principal focus of literary critics is on the task of interpretation, critics sometimes find themselves advocating for new or ignored writers and texts. Critics play the role of cultural gatekeepers, championing some works as "legitimate" subjects of scholarly interpretation and discussion. *Example:* "The writing of Stephen Crane seeks to construct and legitimize a West that is both innocent and knowing, a double vision that converges in the town of Yellow Sky."

map (as a verb): Texts are typically talked about in spatial terms: we read meaning "into" the text; we get meaning "out of" a text; we read "deeply" with "insight," etc. Similarly, the notion of a text as a three-dimensional experience extends to the way meaning may be said to be "mapped." *Example:* "In each of the four sections, key references to the outsider map important sites of meaning."

marginalize: Over the last decade or so, critics have become particularly interested in forms of representation that seem outside the accepted literary canon—vernacular art forms, diaries, travel literature, folk art, and so on. For many young critics, the margin is where the critical action happens. *Example:* "Once marginalized as pulp fiction and seen as unimportant or vulgar by members of the cultural elite, the Western is now regarded as a genre of central cultural significance."

mediate (with a text rather than a negotiator as the subject of the sentence, and often taking a direct object): Like the term "negotiate" below, "mediate" suggests that literary texts may function both aesthetically and socially. *Example:* "Short stories such as 'The Bride Comes to Yellow Sky' attempt to mediate a space between marginal and mainstream cultural values."

negotiate (applied to strategies or ideas rather than treaties): This word has become a verb of choice in dealing with ideas and interpretations, especially for those critics committed to reader-response and cultural criticism. The verb (which is also a metaphor) suggests that there is no single (or simple) truth extractable from the text, that meanings are worked out through discussion and disagreement. *Example:* "The meaning of a story is seldom singular and never static; it is something that must be negotiated with each new reading."

privilege (with a direct object): A term suggesting that, as critics, we consciously or unconsciously give priority to certain issues, genres, and authors. *Example:* "For generations university English departments have privileged expressions of 'high' culture, such as poetry, over more popular genres, such as magazines, romance novels, and Westerns."

problematize (often, though not always, with a direct object): A frequently used term—but one that tends to annoy some traditionalists—*problematize* accentuates the critic's fascination with complexity as a literary value. *Example:* "A character such as Scratchy Wilson acts to problematize notions of good and evil in the mind of the reader."

reading (as a noun): As one might expect in a field that pays so much attention to the reading process, the word "reading" has become synonymous with "interpretation." *Example:* "Katherine Sutherland offers a distinctly feminist reading of 'The Bride Comes to Yellow Sky.'"

reconfigure: This term provides another spatial metaphor, this one associated with the way we structure knowledge. "Reconfigure" suggests that, with some critical effort, we can reposition ourselves and thus rearrange our understandings of the text. *Example:* "The presence of the 'foreign condition' (marriage) forces both Potter and Wilson to adjust and thus reconfigure their understanding of the world around them."

situate: Another spatial term, "situate" implicitly acknowledges that all knowledge (including interpretation) is situated in a particular historical and cultural time and place. *Example:* "It is useful to situate our reading in a historical as well as a literary context."

subvert (typically with a direct object): Talk of subversion reflects critical concern for the dynamics of the reading experience, characterizing textual patterns in oppositional terms. *Example:* "The reference to some Jewish women in the East Side of New York acts to subvert any illusion that the new, industrial East is necessarily more hospitable to women than the Old West."

theorize (often with a direct object): This term emphasizes the importance of literary theory generally. *Example:* "The discourse of colonialism has now been very extensively theorized."

Resources for Further Study

Some Recommended Books, Essays, and Sources on Literary Theory and Critical Approaches

Good Places to Begin

Barry, Peter. *Beginning Theory: An Introduction to Literary and Cultural Theory*. Manchester: Manchester UP, 2002. Print.

Bressler, Charles E. *Literary Criticism: An Introduction to Theory and Practice*. 3rd ed. Upper Saddle River, NJ: Prentice Hall, 2003. Print.

Culler, Jonathan. *Literary Theory: A Very Short Introduction*. New York: Oxford UP, 2011. Print.

Hicks, Malcolm, and Bill Hutchings. *Literary Criticism: A Practical Guide for Students*. London: Edward Arnold, 1989. Print.

Lynn, Steven. "A Passage into Critical Theory." *College English* 52 (1990): 258–71. Print.

Neel, Jasper P. "Writing about Literature (or Country Ham)." *Publishing in English Education*. Ed. Stephen Judy. Montclair, NJ: Boynton/Cook, 1982. 53–72. Print.

Seldon, Raman. *A Reader's Guide to Contemporary Literary Theory*. 2nd ed. Lexington: UP of Kentucky, 1989. Print.

For More In-Depth (and Frequently Cited) Material on Critical Theory and Critical Practices

Abrams, M.H. *The Mirror and the Lamp: Romantic Theory and the Critical Tradition*. Oxford and New York: Oxford UP, 1953. Print.

Bleich, David. *Subjective Criticism*. Baltimore: Johns Hopkins UP, 1978. Print.

Coe, Richard, Lorelei Lingard, and Tatiana Teslenko, eds. *The Rhetoric and Ideology of Genre: Strategies for Stability and Change*. Cresskill, NJ: Hampton Press, 2002. Print.

Empson, William. *Seven Types of Ambiguity*. 2nd ed. London: Chatto and Windus, 1947. Print.

Fish, Stanley. *Is There a Text in This Class? The Authority of Interpretive Communities*. Cambridge, MA: Harvard UP, 1980. Print.

Frye, Northrop. *Anatomy of Criticism: Four Essays.* 1957. Princeton, NJ: Princeton UP, 2000. Print.

Irigaray, Luce. *Speculum of the Other Woman.* Ithaca, NY: Cornell UP, 1985. Print.

Johnson, Barbara. *The Critical Difference: Essays in the Contemporary Rhetoric of Reading.* Baltimore: Johns Hopkins UP, 1980. Print.

Lentricchia, Frank, and Thomas McLaughlin. *Critical Terms for Literary Study.* Chicago: U of Chicago P, 1990. Print.

Patai, Daphne, and Will H. Corral. *Theory's Empire: An Anthology of Dissent.* New York: Columbia UP, 2005. Print.

Richter, David H. *Falling into Theory: Conflicting Views on Reading Literature.* Boston: Bedford Books, 1994. Print.

Scholes, Robert. *Textual Power: Literary Theory and the Teaching of English.* New Haven, CT: Yale UP, 1985. Print.

Sedgwick, Eve Kosofsky. *Epistemology of the Closet.* 2nd ed. Berkeley: U of California P, 2008. Print.

Showalter, Elaine, ed. *The New Feminist Criticism: Essays on Women, Literature and Theory.* London: Virago, 1986. Print.

Tompkins, Jane P., ed. *Reader-Response Criticism: From Formalism to Post-Structuralism.* Baltimore: Johns Hopkins UP, 1980. Print.

Veeser, H. Aram, ed. *The New Historicism.* New York: Routledge, 1989. Print.

For Information on the History and Philosophy of the Field

Eagleton, Terry. *After Theory.* New York: Basic Books, 2003. Print.

———. *Literary Theory: An Introduction.* 2nd ed. Minneapolis: U of Minnesota P, 1996. Print.

Elbow, Peter. *What is English?* New York: Modern Language Association of America, 1990. Print.

Graff, Gerald. *Professing Literature: An Institutional History.* Chicago: U of Chicago P, 1987. Print.

Hubert, Henry A. *Harmonious Perfection: The Development of English Studies in Nineteenth-Century Anglo-Canadian Colleges.* East Lansing: Michigan State UP, 1994. Print.

Johns, Ann M. *Text, Role, and Context: Developing Academic Literacies.* Cambridge: Cambridge UP, 1997. Print.

Murray, Heather. *Working in English: History, Institution, Resources.* Toronto: U of Toronto P, 1996. Print.

Internet Resources

Listservs (electronic discussion lists of interest to the student critic)

The Voice of the Shuttle Website offers an excellent compilation of literature listservs: <http://vos.ucsb.edu/browse.asp?id=2976>

There are hundreds of discussion lists available. Ask your instructor for other recommended listservs.

Sites Worth Visiting

Voice of the Shuttle:
  <http://vos.ucsb.edu/browse.asp?id=3>
A video introduction to literary theory by Yale professor Paul H. Fry, via Academic Earth:
  <http://www.academicearth.org/lectures/intro-literary-theory-1/>
English Literature on the Web: a Hyper-Concordance:
  <http://www.lang.nagoya-u.ac.jp/~matsuoka/EngLit.html>
The Victorian Web:
  <http://www.victorianweb.org/>

These four sites will provide gateways to a wealth of information on writing and literary criticism:

Purdue University's On-Line Writing Lab:
  <http://owl.english.purdue.edu>
E-Server is a digital humanities site based at Iowa State University:
  <http://eserver.org/>
Literary Resources on the Web:
  <http://andromeda.rutgers.edu/%7Ejlynch/Lit/>
Concordia University Library Guide to MLA Referencing Style:
  <http://library.concordia.ca/help/howto/mla.php>

Works Cited

Beach, Richard, and Susan Hynds, eds. *Developing Discourse Practices in Adolescence and Adulthood*. Norwood, NJ: Ablex, 1990. Print.

Birenbaum, Harvey. *The Happy Critic*. Mountain View, CA: Mayfield, 1997. Print.

Burke, Kenneth. *Counter-Statement*. Berkeley: U of California P, 1968. Print.

——. *The Philosophy of Literary Form*. Berkeley: U of California P, 1973. Print.

——. *Terms for Order*. Ed. Stanley Edgar Hyman. Bloomington: Indiana UP, 1964. Print.

Coe, Richard M. "Teaching Genre as Process." *Learning and Teaching Genre*. Ed. Aviva Freedman and Peter Medway. Portsmouth, NH: Boynton/Cook Heinemann, 1994. 157–69. Print.

Copley, Catherine. "Academic Writing Definition." *ESC Online Writing Center*. Empire State College. <http://www.esc.edu/online-writing-center/resources/academic-writing/definition/> Web. 29 Apr. 2012.

Eagleton, Terry. *Literary Theory: An Introduction*. 2nd ed. Cambridge, MA: Blackwell, 1996. Print.

Fahnestock, Jeanne, and Marie Secor. "The Rhetoric of Literary Criticism." *Textual Dynamics of the Professions: Historical and Contemporary Studies of Writing in Professional Communities*. Ed. Charles Bazerman and James Paradis. Madison: U of Wisconsin P, 1991. 76–96. Print.

Fink, Thomas A. "Reading Deconstructively in the Two-Year College Literature Class." *Teaching English in the Two Year College* 12 (Feb. 1985): 64–71. Print.

Frye, Northrop. "The Critical Discipline." *Canadian Universities Today: Symposium Presented to the Royal Society of Canada in 1960*. Ed. George Stanley and Guy Sylvestre. Toronto: U of Toronto P, 1961. 30–37. Print.

Geertz, Clifford. *The Interpretation of Cultures*. New York: Basic Books, 1973. Print.

Giltrow, Janet. *Academic Writing: Writing and Reading Across the Disciplines*. 3rd ed. Peterborough, ON: Broadview P, 2002. Print.

Harris, Robin. *English Studies at Toronto: A History*. Toronto: U of Toronto P, 1988. Print.

Holton, Milne. *Cylinder of Vision: The Fiction and Journalistic Writing of Stephen Crane*. Baton Rouge: Louisiana State UP, 1972. Print.

Hubert, Henry A., and W.F. Garrett-Petts. "Foreword: An Historical Narrative of Textual Studies in Canada." *Textual Studies in Canada* 1 (1991): 1–30. Print.

Hunt, Russell A. "Traffic in Genres, In Classrooms and Out." *Genre and the New Rhetoric*. Ed. Aviva Freedman and Peter Medway. London: Taylor & Francis, 1994. 211–30. Print.

LaFrance, Marston. *A Reading of Stephen Crane*. Oxford: Clarendon Press, 1971. Print.

Lanham, Richard A. "One, Two, Three." *Composition & Literature: Bridging the Gap*. Ed. Winifred Bryan Hornet. Chicago: U of Chicago P, 1983. 14–29. Print.

Lanier, Douglas. "Less Is More: Coverage, Critical Diversity, and the Limits of Pluralism." *Practicing Theory in Introductory College Literature Courses*. Ed. James M. Cahalan and David B. Downing. Urbana, IL: National Council of Teachers of English, 1991. 199–212. Print.

Marius, Richard. "Reflections on the Freshman English Course." *Teaching Literature: What is Needed Now*. Ed. James Engell and David Perkins. Cambridge, MA: Harvard UP, 1988. 169–90. Print.

Monteiro, George. "Crane's 'The Bride Comes to Yellow Sky.'" *Approaches to the Short Story*. Ed. Neil D. Isaacs and Louis H. Leiter. San Francisco: Chandler, 1963. 221–37. Print.

Neel, Jasper. "Dichotomy, Consubstantiality, Technical Writing, Literary Theory: The Double Orthodox Curse." *Journal of Advanced Composition* 12 (Fall 1992): 305–20. Print.

Rabinowitz, Peter. "Our Evaluation of Literature Has Been Distorted by Academe's Bias Toward Close Readings of Texts." *Chronicle of Higher Education* 6 April 1988: A40. Print.

Smith, Frank. *Understanding Reading*. New York: Holt, Rinehart and Winston, 1982. Print.

Index

from the publisher

A name never says it all, but the word "broadview" expresses a good deal of the philosophy behind our company. We are open to a broad range of academic approaches and political viewpoints. We pay attention to the broad impact book publishing and book printing has in the wider world; we began using recycled stock more than a decade ago, and for some years now we have used 100% recycled paper for most titles. As a Canadian-based company we naturally publish a number of titles with a Canadian emphasis, but our publishing program overall is internationally oriented and broad-ranging. Our individual titles often appeal to a broad readership too; many are of interest as much to general readers as to academics and students.

Founded in 1985, Broadview remains a fully independent company owned by its shareholders—not an imprint or subsidiary of a larger multinational.

If you would like to find out more about Broadview and about the books we publish, please visit us at **www.broadviewpress.com**. And if you'd like to place an order through the site, we'd like to show our appreciation by extending a special discount to you: by entering the code below you will receive a 20% discount on purchases made through the Broadview website.

Discount code: **broadview20%**

Thank you for choosing Broadview.

Please note: this offer applies only to sales of bound books within the United States or Canada.

LIST
of products used:

855 lb(s) of Roland Enviro100 Print
100% post-consumer

RESULTS
Based on the Cascades products you selected
compared to products in the industry made with
100% virgin fiber, your savings are:

7 trees

7,073 gal. US of water
77 days of water consumption

894 lbs of waste
8 waste containers

2,324 lbs CO2
4,408 miles driven

11 MMBTU
55,125 60W light bulbs for one hour

7 lbs NOx
**emissions of one truck during 10
days**